# ONCE A CATHOLIC

## Tony Coffey

**HARVEST HOUSE PUBLISHERS**
Eugene, Oregon 97402

**ONCE A CATHOLIC**

Copyright © 1993 by Harvest House Publishers
Eugene, Oregon 97402
Original edition Copyright © 1990 by Tony Coffey

Library of Congress Cataloging-in-Publication Data

Coffey, Tony, 1943-
    Once a Catholic  /  Tony Coffey.
        p.    cm.
    ISBN 1-56507-045-3
    1. Catholic Church—Controversial literature.
    2. Apologetics—20th century.    I. Title.
    BX1765.2.C59      1993
    230'.2—dc20                                    92-45212
                                                   CIP

# With Appreciation

There is a group of dear Christian friends to whom I owe a debt of gratitude. Their assistance in reading the original manuscript and making insightful suggestions is deeply appreciated. To Mick Maguire, one of the firstfruits of our work in Dublin, Graham Fisher (England), and Alastair Ferrie (Scotland) I express my thanks. Thanks also to Dale Paterson (Canada) for gladly taking on the tedious task of line editing for the first edition of this book.

A special word of thanks to my daughter Amy for checking all quotations. Finally to Leslie, not only for having read the manuscript several times, but more importantly, for having introduced me to the living Christ in the Scriptures.

*Dedicated*
*to*
*C. and Louise Burkhart*
*who passed the faith on to the next generation*

# Foreword

I am very pleased to write the foreword to this book. I first met the author when he came to India as part of an evangelistic team. Each evening I attended meetings in which the team members proclaimed the apostolic message. During the time I spent with Tony Coffey the following week, I realized that I had met a sincere evangelist, one who was committed to the authority of the Scriptures and who desired to spread the same gospel preached by the early church. The concept he presented of simply being a Christian—nothing more, nothing less—deeply impressed me as representing what I had always wanted to be.

*Once a Catholic* is of particular interest to me because I was a Catholic priest for 15 years serving in various capacities: parish priest, convent chaplain, vocation promoter, minor seminary professor, director of youth organizations, editor of Catholic journals, author of a number of books, consultor to the Bishop, etc. My reasons for leaving the Catholic Church and its priesthood are best explained in the book you are now reading.

Having spent so many years of my life preaching a message that never set people free, I feel a genuine sadness in my heart for many Catholic friends who are burdened with religious traditions that prevent them from seeing the true meaning of the gospel. Unfortunately, so many of my former beliefs were based upon the teachings of men and not upon the Word of God. I say this as one who spent ten years in training for the priesthood. My prayer is that those who read this book will see the light of the glorious gospel of our Lord and Savior and be saved.

The spirit in which *Once a Catholic* is written is commendable. Writing as one who was previously a Catholic, Tony Coffey writes not out of anger or bitterness, but out of a deep respect for what God says in the Scriptures. His presentation is made in a spirit of respect and love for those of the Roman Catholic faith.

I find great benefit in this book for my own preaching ministry and am pleased to recommend *Once a Catholic* because it seeks to point people to the Lord Jesus Christ, of whom the Scriptures speak.

—Silvester Ezhumala
H.L.M. Centre
Kaloor, Kochi, India
October 1990

# Contents

# Simply Christians

Ever since Pope John XXIII called on the Roman Catholic Church to open the windows and let in the fresh air, a mighty wind has rushed through that Church, bringing many changes to what was perceived as a static institution. The time for the unchanging Church to change had arrived. The documents of the Second Vatican Council grew out of this environment and reflected the new face of Catholicism. The documents were received with enthusiasm by the Catholic world, and nods of approval came from Christian traditions other than Roman Catholic. A new dawn was breaking.

The Papacy also took on a new image. In its long history the Papacy has never enjoyed such a high profile as it does today. No longer is the Pope seen only within the confines of the Vatican; globe-trotting has become part of the Papal duties. The media has given the Papacy celebrity status, and the darker side of its history is almost forgotten.

The Catholic Charismatic Renewal has also made its contribution to the changing face of Catholicism. Whatever misgivings one might have about some aspects of the movement, it must be credited with producing some positive signs. For the first time the Scriptures became a vital part of the lives of many Catholics.

Though the changes in the Catholic Church have been many and favorable, the major issue separating Catholics and Protestants has never been resolved: the authority of the Scriptures in all matters of belief and practice. This unresolved issue has left a yawning gap in its wake. Do we accept the Scriptures alone, or must they be supplemented with tradition? We must make a decision on this issue, since it is impossible for both positions to be correct. Centuries of tradition have formed doctrines unknown by Jesus and his apostles.

I cast my lot with a long and distinguished body of belief that holds the Scriptures to be our only source of authority in all matters religious. The boundaries of our beliefs are determined not by what the Church says, but by what the Scriptures say.

This was not always my view. My early religious heritage was rooted in Catholicism, which brought blessings to my life, though I eventually parted company from Catholicism. In June 1967 my life stood at a spiritual crossroads; I had to make a decision. Would I reject much of what I had been taught as a Catholic, teachings unfounded in Scripture, and instead base my faith on Scripture alone?

The direction I needed to take was clearly marked: "I am the light of the world," Jesus said. "Whoever follows me will never walk in darkness" (John 8:12). If I trusted Jesus completely and followed only what he said, then how could I ever be wrong? And so I began a new life as one of his disciples. That journey has been a joyful experience, though not without its struggles, its hurts, and its pains. But then Jesus never promised any of us a bed of roses.

From the time of my conversion to Jesus I have had the desire to share the gospel with others. My newfound faith was not something I could keep to myself; to have done so would have made me feel like the four lepers who discovered bountiful provisions in the midst of a siege and said, "We're not doing right. This is a day of good news and we are keeping it to ourselves" (2 Kings 7:9). I thank God that he has kept alive in me both the desire and the urgency to share the gospel with others.

*Once a Catholic* is written for Catholics. In writing for a Catholic audience I recognize how easy it would be to give needless offense and become insensitive to the sincere beliefs of others. Because of this, I have tried repeatedly to put myself in the place of the reader and ask, "What would this book have to have in order for me to keep reading it?" It was not hard to come up with the right answers. To keep my attention the book would have to be grounded in Scripture, not opinion. And the writer would need to display a kind and respectful spirit in dealing with doctrines that are sincerely believed by many. Above all, I would want the writer to show a loyalty to the Lord Jesus Christ and a holy jealousy in defending the will of God.

I have tried to do just that. I know that not everyone who reads this book will agree with me. Some will be offended at what I say. Others will read this book with their minds already made up, so that nothing I say will change them. That discourages me. However, there are others whose lives will be blessed. Their eyes will be opened to the wonderful truths of the Scriptures and they will find their every need being met in Jesus Christ alone.

One real difficulty I faced in writing this book was trying to present the beliefs of Catholics, for not all Catholics believe exactly the same doctrine, and some are quite selective in what they believe. The span of persons covers the average lay Catholic to the theologian. For example, there are areas of theology under constant review, and dialogue is carried on with Christians in traditions other than Roman Catholic. The result has been the publication of a number of agreed statements of various doctrines, but the official teaching of the Catholic Church has remained unchanged. For that reason I have restricted myself to quoting only official documents on Roman Catholic doctrine. I am well aware that some readers will not accept these, regarding them as outdated; however, these are still the official teaching of the Roman Catholic Church.

There are two fears I have about this book.

First, it might be used in a manner never intended. *Once a Catholic* has not been written to fuel the fires of sectarianism or to provide ammunition for overzealous persons who delight in scoring cheap points at the expense of the beliefs of others. I want to distance myself from those who engage in such unholy warfare. Second, I fear that some people will see this book only in a negative light, as being out of touch with the ecumenical climate of the day. The idea of refuting the beliefs of another person is seen as belonging to the distant past.

But controversy surrounded the life and teachings of Christ. He frequently collided with the religious establishment, refuting their beliefs and practices. Much of what they believed was based on tradition and was hopelessly adrift from the Word of God. Was Jesus wrong to point out their error? Of course not.

Was the apostle Paul wrong in defending the gospel when it was being undermined by religious traditions? So strong was his denunciation of those who preached another gospel that his words would give offense to many people today:

> Even if we or an angel from heaven should preach a gospel other than the one we preached to you, let him be eternally condemned! As we have already said, so now I say again: If anybody is preaching to you a gospel other than what you accepted, let him be eternally condemned! (Galatians 1:8,9).

Strong words indeed! But thank God for men like Paul who are more interested in defending the saving message of Jesus than in enjoying the approval of the religious establishment.

I feel comfortable knowing that throughout this book I point people to Jesus and encourage them to build their faith on the solid foundation of his teachings. Surely that cannot be wrong! In fact, it is exactly what the Lord wants us to do:

> Everyone who hears these words of mine and puts them into practice is like a wise man who built his house on the rock. The rain came down, the streams rose, the winds blew and beat against the house; yet it did not fall, because it had its foundations on the rock. But everyone who hears

these words of mine and does not put them into
practice is like a foolish man who built his house
on sand. The rain came down, the streams rose,
and the winds blew and beat against that house,
and it fell with a great crash (Matthew 7:24-27).

The written word has its limitations, as the apostle Paul
knew only too well. Paul said some hard but necessary
words to the Christians in Galatia, but then hastened to ask
them, "Have I now become your enemy by telling you the
truth?" Yet he didn't stop there. He wanted them to know
that the truth he shared came from someone who deeply
cared about them, so he continued, "How I wish I could be
with you now and change my tone . . ." (Galatians 4:16,20).

I too have had that apostolic feeling while writing this
book. I wish I could be with you to answer your questions
in a more direct way. I want you to hear that my replies
come from a heart filled with the conviction that if we
follow Jesus Christ, we will never be lost. In our walk with
the Lord we will be neither Catholics nor Protestants; we
will simply be Christians just as they were in the early
church. The traditions that have been taken on board over
the centuries can be discarded in favor of the full truth
contained in the inspired Scriptures. If your heart beats a
little faster at the prospect of simply being a Christian—a
member of the body of Christ, the church—then this book
is written for you.

My prayer is that the quest of the Bereans will become
the quest of all Roman Catholics: "The Bereans were of
more noble character than the Thessalonians, for they
received the message with great eagerness and examined
the Scriptures every day to see if what Paul said was true"
(Acts 17:11).

# CHAPTER 1

# Who Speaks for God?

The attitude of Jesus to the Scriptures must be our flagship in life if we are to reach our heavenly destination. Jesus said, "The Scripture cannot be broken" (John 10:35). Such a clear statement should settle for all time that the Scriptures are indeed our only authority in all matters of belief and practice. Obedience to what Scripture says is not optional; it is a command to be obeyed.

Yet many Roman Catholics accept the authority of their Church in addition to and sometimes overriding the Scriptures. The fullness of truth, they maintain, is contained not in Scripture alone, but in both Scripture and tradition. By tradition I mean the teachings of the Catholic Church. These are teachings that do not have their roots in Scripture, but have evolved over many centuries and have finally been defined as dogma by the Church.

## The Final Authority

I left the Catholic Church once I became convinced that the Scriptures alone are the final authority to which we must yield obedience. The shift in my thinking began when I started reading the Scriptures. This was a new experience for me. I was both frightened and excited at what I was doing. I was frightened because I was wading in uncharted waters and going outside the boundaries of where I was told all truth resides: in the Church's official teaching. But I was excited at seeing the simplicity of going back to the Scriptures and simply being a Christian, a member of the body of Christ, the church. The idea of holding to something that never changes made a lot of sense to me, and the Scriptures provided that unchangeable message.

I was reared to believe in the authoritative teaching of the Catholic Church. However, I was becoming continually impressed while reading the four Gospels to see how often Jesus referred only to Scripture and never to tradition when teaching on matters of faith and morals. This was so unlike the practice of the Catholic Church, which appealed to the teachings of Popes, Papal Encyclicals, and tradition, but seldom to Scripture. I concluded that if Jesus accepted only the Scriptures, I would not be wrong if I followed his example.

We can be greatly helped by seeing how Jesus dealt with some of life's important questions. In every case he directed people to the written word of God.

### Jesus and the Scriptures

Our first example involves an expert in the law who came to Jesus with a question. Whether he realized it or not, he was about to ask the most important question a person can ever ask: "What must I do to inherit eternal life?"

That question demanded an authoritative reply, and Jesus supplied it: "What is written in the law?" ... "How do you read it?" (Luke 10:25,26). I am impressed that a question about eternal life is answered by Christ not from tradition but from the Scriptures.

How would the Catholic Church answer the question Jesus was asked? Would they seek the answer in the Scriptures, or would they appeal to an additional source? The appeal would not be to the Scriptures alone, since the

Catholic Church does not believe that the entire will of God is contained in the Scriptures, but that Scripture must be supplemented by the teaching of the Church. The picture, they say, is only complete when Scripture and tradition are presented together. Yet if the same question were asked of Jesus today, he would surely not say, "You must listen to the Catholic Church." Rather, he would point us to the Scriptures alone, as he always did during his earthly ministry.

Our second example is recorded in the Gospel of Luke. On this occasion Jesus told a story of two men, one rich and the other a beggar. The day came when both men died and received their reward. The poor man went to heaven and the rich man was lost in hell. From his place of torment he pleaded for someone to return to his family and tell them how to avoid ending up in the same place. However, his newfound zeal for mission work was really unnecessary, since God had no burning ambition to overpopulate hell. "They have Moses and the Prophets," the rich man was told; "let them listen to them" (Luke 16:29).

While the story has several important lessons, the one that is of greatest interest to us is that the Lord proclaimed the Scriptures (Moses and the Prophets) to be completely sufficient to show a person how to live for God. Jesus is teaching us that there is no need for anyone's family to be lost if they will but listen to what God is saying in the Scriptures. The problem is not that God is silent, but that we are poor listeners.

Our third example in this brief overview of the Lord's use of Scripture occurred after he was raised from the dead. On that Easter Sunday the risen Lord met two of his disciples on the road to the town of Emmaus. His death had emptied their hearts of all joy; their hopes were dashed. In the course of the evening Jesus revealed himself to them: "Beginning with Moses and all the Prophets, he explained to them what was said in all the Scriptures concerning himself" (Luke 24:27). That must have been one fabulous Bible study! No wonder the two disciples said, "Were not our hearts burning within us while he talked with us on the road and opened the Scriptures to us?" (Luke 24:32). In that discussion Jesus would have cited all the major texts in the Scriptures that had reference to his coming into the world and to his work of redemption for each one of us. All these great doctrines were contained not in a body of tradition similar to that in the Catholic Church, but in the Scriptures alone.

Before his ascension Jesus told his disciples, "Everything must be fulfilled that is written about me in the Law of Moses, the Prophets and the Psalms" (Luke 24:44). The point cannot be made strongly enough that Jesus came not to fulfill *tradition* but only what was written about him *in the Scriptures*. Jesus was able to go *to the Scriptures* and from them establish who he was and why he had come into the world. He was able to point to the writings of Moses, Isaiah, Daniel, and David and say, "Here it is; read it for yourself." Why did Jesus have such a high regard for Scripture? Because God's fingerprints could be found on every page of his written Word.

### The Scriptures Are from God

A study of prophecy and its fulfillment has done much to convince people that the Scriptures are indeed from God. For example, how did the prophets who lived centuries before Jesus was born know so much about him? How did they know that he would be born of a virgin in the town of Bethlehem? How did they know that he would grow up in Nazareth? How did they know that he would be betrayed for 30 pieces of silver? How did they know that he would be crucified between two thieves? How did they know that he would be raised from the dead?

Dozens more prophecies could be cited, but these are sufficient to show that there can be only one explanation as to how the prophets could write with such accuracy about events centuries before they occurred: "Prophecy never had its origin in the will of man, but men spoke from God as they were carried along by the Holy Spirit" (2 Peter 1:21). In other words, the prophecies came from God, who communicated them to his prophets, who in turn were guided by the Holy Spirit in recording them in the Scriptures: "All Scripture is God-breathed" (2 Timothy 3:16). What the Old Testament prophesied, the New Testament Scriptures record as having been fulfilled.

The teachings of the Catholic Church could never be reproduced from the Scriptures alone, for by its own admission much of Catholic belief is drawn from both the Scriptures and the teachings of the Church. This admission should cause Catholics to wonder about the claims of a Church whose beliefs are not based entirely on the Word of God. I intend no disrespect, or seek to gain no cheap points, but no one could ever become a Roman Catholic if he followed only what the Bible teaches. One needs the extrabiblical teachings of the Catholic Church to be a Roman Catholic. But when tradition is introduced on an equal footing with the Word of God, the inevitable collision occurs. We must heed the words of Jesus, who said that "the Scripture cannot be broken" (John 10:35). Unfortunately it was not Scripture but the religious traditions of that day that proved to be the great menace to the ministry of our Lord.

## Jesus Versus Tradition

Everywhere Jesus went, controversy erupted with the religious teachers. The cause of it all was their religious traditions. I had often wondered why Jesus was rejected by a religious people. I could understand if he was rejected by pagans, or God-denying atheists who knew no better, but the Jews were a deeply religious people who believed in Jehovah God. It is only when we begin to see that much of their religion was based not on Scripture but on their traditions, and that Jesus continually violated these traditions, that an explanation for his rejection emerges. These traditions were bound upon the people by an influential clergy who were regarded as the official interpreters of God's law.

Though the Scriptures were read in the synagogue every Sabbath, the message never got through to the hearts of the people, for it was first filtered through the traditions of the leaders. This is vividly displayed in one encounter that

Jesus had with the religious teachers. Jesus had just restored a man to full health on the Sabbath, and for this he was taken to task and accused of being a lawbreaker. For the Jews, their traditions had been violated by Jesus. Because he made this sick man well, Jesus was accused of doing work on the Sabbath. According to their interpretation of the law, Jesus' act of charity broke the law.

Yet Jesus not only defended his action by his miracles, but showed his accusers why they were unable to see who he was: God the Son, the One spoken of by all the prophets. Those responsible for rejecting him were the theologians of the day. They were the educated teachers who had studied the ancient Scriptures. But it was the influence of their traditions that had set their minds in concrete, leaving no room for the possibility of further light. "You diligently study the Scriptures," Jesus said to them. "These are the Scriptures that testify about me" (John 5:39).

Two points stand out here: First, they did study the Scriptures, not casually but diligently. Second, the Scriptures they studied referred to Jesus. Yet they failed to believe in Jesus! They had the Scriptures and they witnessed his miracles, but they remained in unbelief. Why? Jesus supplies the answer: "If you believed Moses, you would believe me, for he wrote about me" (John 5:46). This is an astonishing statement because these people claimed to be disciples of Moses and avid readers of his writings, yet they couldn't see that Jesus was the central character in all of Moses' writings. What Jesus was saying to them was, "You don't even believe what you read."

The obstacle that caused their blindness was their religious traditions. Jesus was not what they had expected in a Messiah. Their disappointment had not been based on anything the *Scriptures* had said, but on what their *traditions* were saying about the Messiah. Tradition became the standard by which Jesus was measured. Once Scripture was abandoned as the norm, these leaders were on the slippery slope to trouble. When Scripture is stripped of its authority, then all the reading and studying of the Scriptures will avail nothing.

## Scripture or Tradition?

I have seen how this works and how relevant Jesus' discussion is to our time. Over the years in doing the work of an evangelist I have often discussed the Scriptures with Catholic priests. I recall several times discussing with them the wonder of the cross of Christ and what that means to us: that in his death, Jesus paid the full penalty of all our sins, and that as a result we are now set free, never to face condemnation. Up to this point we would have agreement. Then I would ask, "Since the death of Jesus paid the full penalty for our sins, why is there a need for purgatory?" Without exception the reply would come, "But the Catholic Church teaches. . . ."

No matter how persuasive my arguments would have been from Scripture, no matter how clearly Scripture revealed that Jesus does fully forgive us and that purgatory contradicts the sacrifice of Christ, the answer would always be the same: "But the Catholic Church says. . . ."

The same response was always given when discussing whether or not Jesus had brothers and sisters. I would show that the Scriptures clearly teach that Jesus did have brothers and sisters. The priests would say that this has reference to his cousins. I would then show that the context does not allow such an interpretation, to which they would reply, "But the Catholic Church says. . . ."

Do you see what is happening here? The evidence of Scripture, compelling though it is, is rejected in favor of traditions that are based on the teachings of men, teachings that contradict the message contained in Scripture. What Jesus said of the Jews of his day is applicable to Catholic teaching also: "Their teachings are but rules taught by men. You have let go of the commands of God and are holding on to the traditions of men" (Mark 7:7,8).

## Changing the Laws

The folly of following the teachings of men can be seen by looking at beliefs which Catholics were once obliged to practice, but which are now no longer binding upon them.

These were Church laws, and carried the penalty of sin if they were broken. I recall many of the rules we were obliged to keep under pain of mortal sin. Before receiving Holy Communion on a Sunday, we had to fast from midnight on Saturday. To break your fast and receive Communion was a sin. The same was true regarding eating meat on a Friday. It was sinful to break your fast. Today these laws are no longer in force. They were made by men and have been removed by men, proving that they did not come from God. Yet we were told that to break one of these laws was to sin against God. How could something be a sin yesterday but not a sin today?

The tragedy of tradition is that it blinds people from seeing God. Tradition causes people to become preoccupied with observing rules and doing their religious duty. Religion is turned into an unthinking exercise, an empty ritual, a boring duty with others doing your thinking for you. Is it any wonder that Jesus exposed tradition? He did this by performing miracles on the Sabbath, thereby breaking religious tradition and kicking a lot of sacred cows. The conflict he experienced is seen in the account of the blind man whose sight he restored on the Sabbath. In order to get the impact of what happened, I will briefly sketch a short history of the Sabbath.

The Sabbath was given to the Jews to commemorate their deliverance from Egypt (Deuteronomy 5:15), and they were charged with keeping that day holy by abstaining from work (Exodus 20:8-11). Over the centuries the teaching authorities had drawn up a long list of do's and don't's regarding Sabbath observance. These rules were viewed as expressing the will of God and were enforced by the religious authorities. So when Jesus worked miracles on the Sabbath he was denounced as a sinner, a violator of God's law, because his miracles were viewed as work, and one didn't work on the Sabbath.

### Healing the Blind

Did Jesus really break the Sabbath? Of course not. What

he broke was man-made traditions which produced a religion that was joyless. No wonder he said that these teachers "load people down with burdens they can hardly carry" (Luke 11:46).

On the Sabbath Jesus restored the sight of a man who had been born blind. The occasion was marked not with celebration but with a public outcry: The Sabbath had been broken. The authorities were quick on the scene and issued an immediate statement: "This man is not from God, for he does not keep the Sabbath."

They conducted an extensive inquiry of the blind man and his parents. "Is this your son?" they asked. "Is this the one you say was born blind? How is it that now he can see?" Frightened, the parents replied, "Ask him. He is of age; he will speak for himself." The parents replied in this sheepish fashion "because they were afraid of the Jews, for already the Jews had decided that anyone who acknowledged that Jesus was the Christ would be put out of the synagogue."

No one could deny that a miracle had indeed occurred, so what were the authorities to do about it? What official statement would they issue to put the minds of the masses at ease? They said, "We know this man is a sinner." To add a touch of respectability to their comments they declared, "We are disciples of Moses! We know that God spoke to Moses, but as for this fellow, we don't even know where he comes from."

When the blind man heard what they said, not only were his eyes wide open, but so was his mouth: "Now that is remarkable! You don't know where he comes from, yet he opened my eyes. . . . If this man were not from God, he could do nothing."

"You were steeped in sin at birth; how dare you lecture us!" they replied as they threw him out (John 9:16-34). Excommunicated!

Here was a miracle which no one could deny: A blind man had been given sight. Yet instead of rejoicing and celebrating the presence of God among them, the religious leaders cast out the blind man and heaped slander upon Jesus. Now why did they do this? Why did they not see the divine evidence of God in the miracle? It was their *traditions* that blinded them. Holding as they did that their traditions were the will of God, they couldn't entertain the possibility that they just might be wrong. Yet the miracle which they could not deny should have caused them to reconsider their position.

Yet to have taken them to the Scriptures and shown them that the Scriptures did in fact speak of Jesus would have been a waste of time. They would have responded, "How could the Scriptures endorse Jesus, since he keeps none of our traditions, including the proper observance of the Sabbath? If he were from God we would know it, for his beliefs would be the same as ours!" When they were pressed for an explanation as to how Jesus was able to work miracles, something which they could not deny, they simply said that he was in league with the devil (Matthew 12:22-32).

Despite the evidence before them the authorities remained in their entrenched position, taking comfort that there had been no defections from their ranks. This was the reply they gave when the soldiers returned without Jesus:

> "Why didn't you bring him in?" "No one ever spoke the way this man does," the guards declared. "You mean he has deceived you also?" the Pharisees retorted. "Has any of the rulers or of the Pharisees believed in him?" (John 7:45-48).

That line of reasoning was intended to deal a fatal blow to the claim that Jesus was the Christ of whom the Scriptures spoke. If Jesus was really the Messiah, they reasoned, wouldn't we have recognized him? I can almost hear them say, "We didn't spend all those years studying the Scriptures for nothing." Is it any wonder that Jesus spoke of them as the blind leading the blind?

### The Teaching Church

It would be inconceivable to think that Jesus came and fulfilled all that the Scriptures had foretold, then ascended to heaven without leaving any means by which the gospel would be proclaimed to all the world. Jesus not only left the message of the gospel, but he also left the messenger to proclaim that gospel—namely, his church. The church is a teaching church charged with telling the good news to the lost and maturing the people of God in the Christian faith.

How does the Catholic Church define its role as a teaching Church? Does it teach only what the Scriptures teach, or does it incorporate the traditions of the Church on an equal footing with Scripture?

> Hence there exist a close connection and communication between sacred tradition and sacred Scripture. . . . Sacred tradition and sacred Scripture form one sacred deposit of the word of God, which is committed to the Church. . . . The test of authentically interpreting the word of God whether written or handed on has been entrusted exclusively to the living teaching office of the Church. It is clear, therefore, that sacred tradition and sacred Scripture, and the teaching authority of the Church, in accord with God's most wise design, are so linked and joined together that one cannot stand without the others, and that all together and each in its own way under the action of the one Holy Spirit contribute effectively to the salvation of souls.[1]
>
> Q.29. Does the Catholic Church derive all her doctrines solely from the Bible?
> No. While most of the Church's teachings are contained in the Bible, some others are not.[2]

Are these statements compatible with the beliefs and practices of the early church which we read about in the Scriptures?

If ever a group of people knew exactly what the Lord intended his church to be, it was the apostles, since they were directly involved in its beginnings. How did they see the church fulfilling its teaching role in the world? What do the Scriptures tell us about the early church? Let's first look at the steps taken by the Lord to ensure that after his departure his church would be equipped to continue his work in the world. We will then look at how the church taught the gospel to the lost and matured the believers in the faith.

The apostles accompanied Jesus throughout most of his public ministry, during which time he was training them for their future work. Indispensable to their ministry was the Holy Spirit, whom Jesus promised to send. Jesus said that when the Spirit came he would "teach you all things and will remind you of everything I have said to you. . . . He will guide you into all truth" (John 14:26; 16:13).

I am impressed by seeing how the early church fulfilled its role of teaching the gospel. The church never held itself forth as the authority to be obeyed. Rather, the church taught people what the *Scriptures* were saying.

### Evangelism in Action

With the coming of the Holy Spirit, evangelism got under way. The first Pentecost Sunday after the resurrection marks the birth of the church of God. On that day the Spirit came and empowered the apostles to teach the gospel, resulting in the conversion of some 3000 people to the Lord (Acts 2:1-47). What converted these people? It certainly wasn't the eloquent speech of the apostles. Reading the second chapter of Acts, we see that the apostles argued their case for Christ not by saying, "The Church says," but by directing people to the truth contained in the Scriptures. These people became the people of God because they believed what God said in the Scriptures. And the church fulfilled its teaching role by instructing people in what the Scriptures had to say. From the beginning the church was a teaching church engaged in teaching only what God had said in the Scriptures.

Stephen, the first Christian martyr, is an example. He was stoned to death by his fellow Jews after surveying the Scriptures in an attempt to show that Jesus was the promised Messiah, the Savior of the world. Like the apostles, he too taught the people only from the Scriptures (Acts 7:1-60). With the tide turning against the church a wave of persecution descended upon the believers. Uprooted from their homes, they continued their evangelism. "Those who had been scattered preached the word wherever they went" (Acts 8:4). What do you think these people preached? It couldn't have been anything to do with tradition, since such a body of belief didn't come into existence until several centuries later. What they preached was the good news that God's promise for forgiveness through Jesus Christ as set forth in the Scriptures is freely available to all.

Evangelism went into overdrive with the conversion of Saul of Tarsus, later known as the apostle Paul. A gifted man with a zeal for God and a love for the lost, Paul succeeded in extending the boundaries of the kingdom of God. Through his tireless efforts many people were converted and the church was being established in cities throughout the world. Paul's starting place for his evangelism was often among his fellow Jews, and the source of his message was always the Scriptures. Surely any claim to being the true church founded by Christ must have the same practice as Paul: an unswerving fidelity to the authority of the Scriptures.

Listen to Luke's words as he records how Paul evangelized: "As his custom was, Paul went into the synagogue, and on three Sabbath days he reasoned with them from the Scriptures, explaining and proving that the Christ had to suffer and rise from the dead. 'This Jesus I am proclaiming to you is the Christ,' he said" (Acts 17:2,3). Where did Paul argue his case from—Scripture or tradition? On another occasion Paul "vigorously refuted the Jews in public debate, proving from the Scriptures that Jesus was the Christ" (Acts 18:28). The evidence that Paul called upon was that body of truth known as the Scriptures.

While under house arrest in Rome, many people were coming to Paul inquiring about the Christ he was preaching. How did Paul deal with their inquiries? "From morning till evening he explained and declared to them the kingdom of God and tried to convince them about Jesus

from the Law of Moses and from the Prophets" (Acts 28:23)
In his own defense Paul said, "I am saying nothing beyond
what the prophets and Moses said would happen" (Acts
26:22).

In other words, Paul never went outside Scripture. Scripture was his only point of reference. Paul, who received his
ministry by way of a revelation from Jesus himself, knew
absolutely nothing of a teaching church which in itself was
the authority. The true teaching church pointed people
only to what was found in Scripture. That is why the
Bereans were commended, "for they received the message
with great eagerness and examined the Scriptures every
day to see if what Paul said was true" (Acts 17:11). Scripture
was the catechism of the early church, and not only figured
prominently in the church's role of teaching the gospel to
the lost, but also in bringing the people of God to spiritual
maturity.

## Spiritual Maturity

What provision did Jesus make to ensure that those who
embraced the Christian faith would be brought to spiritual
maturity? Just as the church was charged with teaching the
gospel to the lost, the church would also be the vehicle
through which Jesus would minister to the needs of his
people, whether they lived in the first century or the twen-
tieth century. The church of Christ is a teaching church,
endowed by Christ with the inspired Scriptures and gifted
teachers to expound these Scriptures.

Scripture provides us with a wonderful picture of Christ
as a victorious warrior who has triumphed over death and
bestows the necessary gifts to his church to sustain her for
all time. These gifts are teaching gifts and come in the form
of apostles, prophets, evangelists, pastors, and teachers. It
is through their ministry that the people of God in all ages
are brought to maturity in Christ Jesus (Ephesians 4:11-16).

The apostles and prophets have a unique ministry in the
church in that through them the complete will of God was
revealed. The early Christians "devoted themselves to the
apostles' teaching" (Acts 2:42). These teachings revealed to

the apostles by the Holy Spirit are the foundation upon which the church is built in every generation (Ephesians 2:20; 3:5).

Since the apostles would not live forever, God made provision to have their teachings permanently preserved in the New Testament Scriptures. When the writings of the apostles and prophets emerged, the church held them as sacred, just as they had the writings of Moses, David, Isaiah, Jeremiah, etc. The same Holy Spirit who had revealed to the apostles the will of God also guided them in the recording of the Scriptures: "All Scripture is God-breathed" (2 Timothy 3:16). Because the New Testament Scriptures were authoritative, having been produced by the Holy Spirit, they were accepted by the church and enjoyed the same status as the Old Testament Scriptures. They too were read in public when the church assembled (Colossians 4:16; Revelation 1:11,19,20; cf. Luke 4:16,17; Acts 13:15).

## Evangelists and Pastors

Evangelists are gifted teachers whom the Lord continually gives to his church. Through them the Lord ministers to his people. Timothy was an evangelist used by God in a very fruitful ministry, proving invaluable to Paul and to the church in general. For example, when the church in the city of Corinth was undergoing problems, it was Timothy whom Paul sent to instruct them in the things he had previously taught them (1 Corinthians 4:17). The work undertaken by Timothy was ordained of God, and Paul reminded the Corinthian church that Timothy was "carrying on the work of the Lord, just as I am" (1 Corinthians 16:10). The work of the Lord for his church today is still being carried out by those whom God has called to be evangelists.

Pastors are also a teaching gift from Christ to the church and are charged with the responsibility of caring for the local church which God has placed in their charge. Just as a shepherd cares for his sheep, pastors are to care for the flock of God, and will account to God for their pastoral ministry (1 Peter 5:1-4; Hebrews 13:17).

How do evangelists and pastors fulfill their ministry to the church of Christ today? Theirs is a ministry that involves the teaching of God's will as set forth in the Scriptures. I have shown several examples of how the early church evangelized through teaching what the Scriptures foretold. And the church today teaches its members by a faithful adherence to what God has revealed in the Scriptures. There is no issue facing us today which is not addressed in God's Word. Whether marriage, divorce, abortion, sex outside marriage, sex within marriage, homosexuality, morals, attitude toward the poor, forgiveness, the church, heaven, or hell, all of these subjects and many more are addressed in the Scriptures. Where an issue is not specifically addressed, sufficient principles are provided in Scripture to give us necessary guidance.

The Catholic Church, on the other hand, has come up with positions that directly contradict Scripture. It is the work of evangelists and pastors to exercise their teaching gifts so that the people of God will "no longer be infants, tossed back and forth by the waves, and blown here and there by every wind of teaching and by the cunning craftiness of men in their deceitful scheming" (Ephesians 4:14).

Jesus ensured that his gospel would be proclaimed and that his church would have the biblical means of attaining spiritual maturity. In both cases the church is the instrument in the hands of God. The Lord has given to his church teachers whom he has endowed with ability to fulfill his will. The church is not an authority on equal footing with the Scriptures, as is taught by the Catholic Church. Rather, the church fulfills its role as a teaching church when evangelists and pastors teach the lost and nurture the saved from the message of God in the Scriptures.

### The Scripture-Based Voice

The church has been given a voice by God to speak on his behalf both to the people of God and to those outside his kingdom. Because of her role she is called "the pillar and the foundation of the truth" (1 Timothy 3:15). How does the church fulfill her mission? Let us look at the church in action in the first century and then move on to the present.

Not long after the church was established it faced its first encounter with heresy. How did the church tackle this problem? We read in Acts 15 that the apostles and the elders of the church met and discussed the problem and arrived at a sound conclusion. Their verdict was circulated among the churches.

The problem they needed to resolve concerned the gospel. Some were saying that people could not become part of God's church unless they first became Jews. This was a denial of the power of the gospel to save people irrespective of their nationality. The conclusion the church arrived at was based upon all that God had revealed, both to the apostles and through the prophets in the Old Testament Scriptures. The message was clear: The gospel alone is sufficient to save people; nothing else is needed for those who come to faith in Christ Jesus. The church's verdict was not a new dogma that became binding upon the people of God; the church was simply restating what God had already said on many occasions. The voice of the church must be heeded when it is accurately declaring what God has said in his Word.

The role of the church today is no different: It must speak for God from his Word. Many pressing questions today must be answered. Whether on abortion, unmarried couples living together, infidelity in marriage, homosexuality, evasion of paying income tax, etc., the church must speak from God's Word on every issue. Not every problem will have a simple solution, and there must be diligent study of the Scriptures and fervent prayer to God for guidance and wisdom. Only as the teaching of the church is gathered from within the boundaries of God's written Word is the church speaking with the authority of God.

# CHAPTER 2

# Who Gave Us the Bible?

*H*ow did the Bible that sits on your bookshelf come into existence? The Catholic Church maintains that it gave us the Bible, that it determined the number of books which should compose the canon of Scripture, in particular the New Testament Scriptures. The argument goes like this: The Church existed before a word of the New Testament Scriptures was written; after they were written, the Church determined the canon; therefore, the Church is the authoritative voice that must be obeyed, for without the Church we would not have the Bible.

### The Catholic Claim

Q. 17 Who can determine what books make up the Bible?

Just as Christ's infallible Church alone can assure us that the Bible is divinely inspired, so the Church alone possesses the authority to indicate what books are included in it.[1]

The Church came into being before the New Testament and it is as a result of this that she

claims to be the final arbiter in matters of interpretation. It was the Church which collected
together the books and letters which make up the
New Testament. She decided what was to be
included and what was to be left out. Thus as the
author of this collection the Church is in a better
position than the reader to say what is meant by a
particular passage.[2]

This argument sounds good and reasonable, but is it
correct? Is the Bible a product of the Catholic Church? Or
did it come into existence in some other way? One could be
forgiven for dismissing the question as being irrelevant,
maintaining that the important thing is that we have the
Bible. But it is not as simple as that. The Catholic claim is
that by its authority we have the Bible, and therefore it
alone is the official interpreter of the Scriptures; if we want
to know the true meaning of Scripture, we must listen to
the Church that gave us the Bible.

Does the evidence support the Catholic claim, or does it
point us in a different direction? We will take our first step
toward answering this question by looking at how the Old
Testament came into existence and at the criteria that determined its canon.

## The Old Testament Canon

Jesus endorsed the 39 books that compose the Old Testament Scriptures as being the authentic Word of God. These
were the Scriptures he had come to fulfill. His "imprima-
tur" had been placed upon them. After his resurrection
Jesus met with his disciples to inform them of all that had
been written about him in the Scriptures: "Beginning with
Moses and all the Prophets, he explained to them what was
said in all the Scriptures concerning himself" (Luke 24:27).

What conclusion can we draw from Jesus' words? Since
the Lord had come to fulfill all that was written about him
in the Scriptures, there had to have existed a recognized
canon of Scripture. How did these 39 books which compose the Old Testament come into existence?

The Old Testament came together quite simply. The main criterion in determining whether a book should be included in the canon pertained to its author. Prophetic authorship was essential. If the author were known to be a prophet of God, his works were preserved. This was obviously at the direction of God.

Moses was a prophet of God, used by him in a mighty way. To ensure that we would have a permanent record of God's revelation, Moses wrote down all that the Lord told him. Furthermore, he placed his writings in a place of honor—next to the ark of the covenant, where God was specially present among his people. "After Moses finished writing in a book the words of this law from beginning to end, he gave this command to the Levites who carried the ark of the covenant of the Lord, 'Take this Book of the Law and place it beside the ark of the covenant of the Lord your God' " (Deuteronomy 31:24-26).

Joshua succeeded Moses as Israel's leader and was a man "filled with the spirit of wisdom because Moses had laid his hands on him" (Deuteronomy 34:9). At the end of his life Joshua added another link to the chain by what he wrote in that he "recorded these things in the Book of the Law of God" (Joshua 24:26). The Old Testament was beginning to take shape.

Samuel is among the outstanding prophets in Israel's history, and he too took pen to paper: "He wrote them down on a scroll and deposited it before the Lord" (1 Samuel 10:25). Note the special place of honor given the Scripture: "before the Lord." Furthermore, "as for the events of King David's reign, from beginning to end, they are written in the records of Samuel the seer" (1 Chronicles 29:29). The prophet Nathan also made his contribution to the formation of the Old Testament: "As for the other events of Solomon's reign, from beginning to end, are they not written in the records of Nathan the prophet?" (2 Chronicles 9:29).

When Israel was faced with 70 years of captivity in Babylon, Daniel was able to turn to the writings of the prophet Jeremiah and see that God had foretold of this time. Daniel "understood from the Scriptures, according to the word of the Lord given to Jeremiah the prophet, that the desolation of Jerusalem would last seventy years" (Daniel 9:2; Jeremiah 29:10).

The prophets wrote on a wide variety of events in the history of God's chosen people, but there was one central theme to their writings: the coming of Jesus Christ the Savior of the world. Jesus maintained that he was the central figure spoken of in the Scriptures. Therefore, "beginning with Moses and all the Prophets, he explained to them what was said in all the Scriptures concerning himself" (Luke 24:27).

Peter in his epistle says that the Old Testament prophecies fulfilled by Jesus provide ample proof that he is the Son of God and that the Scriptures give us all the assurance and guidance we need (2 Peter 1:12-21). Peter is saying that we do not need to go outside of what Scripture says.

What have we said so far? *The Old Testament was accepted by the people of God because it was written by the prophets of God.* The writings of the prophets were preserved because of their divine origin. Though the people of God were involved in gathering these sacred writings, this never gave them a position of authority over (or even equal with) the Scriptures. By the time Jesus came, the canon (the recognized collection of books) in the Old Testament had been established and had received the endorsement of Christ himself. These were the Scriptures that Jesus appealed to during his ministry, maintaining that the central message of the Old Testament spoke of his coming to save us from our sins and to bring us back to the Father. In contrast to this, the message of the New Testament records the fulfillment of all that Jesus accomplished. The Old Testament was written over a period of 1500 years. The New Testament Scriptures were written within a 60-year period.

## The New Testament Canon

By the close of the first century, the 27 books that compose the New Testament had been accepted by the early church as canonical. The evidence for this is verified by early church history. (For those wishing a more thorough treatment of this subject, I list several books for further reference at the end of this chapter.)

The Catholic Church maintains that the collection of books that should compose the New Testament canon was determined at the Council of Carthage in A.D. 397. This is incorrect. The purpose of this Council was not to sort through old dusty scrolls that had been stored in some monastic attic and then announce to the Christian world which books were canonical and which were not. The Council simply affirmed what the early church had long since accepted—the particular 27 books that compose the New Testament.

We must not make the mistake of thinking that the Scriptures received their authority because some council made a public statement of their acceptance. The truth of the matter is that the early church accepted the Scriptures because it believed them to be from God and saw itself as subject to their authority, and not the other way around. Though the church existed before the New Testament was written, this does not give the church authority over the Scriptures or even authority equal to that of the Scriptures. The church must always be subject to the authority of God's written Word.

What enabled the church to accept the canon of the New Testament so readily was the unique position of the apostles. They were the Lord's companions for most of his ministry, and he trained them for a special mission: world evangelism. Not only were they eyewitnesses to the resurrection of Jesus, but they were endowed with the necessary credentials to establish themselves as God's spokespersons. The miracles they performed testified to this role. We read that "the apostles performed many miraculous signs and wonders among the people" (Acts 5:12). This included raising the dead to life and restoring the sick to perfect health. Further confirmation was given to the apostolic ministry in that "God did extraordinary miracles through Paul" (Acts 19:11). Paul had no hesitation in pointing to the miracles performed by the apostles as proof of their divine calling (2 Corinthians 12:12).

For many years the apostles taught the church all that God was revealing to them, and the church accepted their teaching. The church had every confidence that what the apostles taught them was indeed the will of God. The apostolic miracles bore further testimony to their mission. Like the prophets before them, they too would die, but God had taken steps to ensure that his message would always be available. The Holy Spirit inspired the apostles to record God's will in the Scriptures, and the church had no difficulty in accepting the writings of Peter or Paul or John. After all, these men had simply committed to written form the great doctrines and morals they had been teaching the church all along.

We must remember that Jesus gave the apostles the very words the Father had given him (John 17:8), and he promised to send the Holy Spirit to teach them, guide them, and recall to their minds all that he had told them during his earthly ministry (John 14:26; 16:13). Part of the Spirit's guidance pertained to the writing of the New Testament. This should not be at all surprising, since the early church grew out of a Jewish heritage, which had accumulated the writings of God's former spokespersons. Under the Spirit's guidance, the early church followed the same practice.

### The Words Preserved

It was inevitable that the writings of the apostles would be preserved, since they contained the fulfillment of all that the prophets had foretold about Jesus. Peter in his epistle gave a generous hint that this process was happening even while he was alive; he saw his writings being permanently available: "I will make every effort to see that after my departure you will always be able to remember these things" (2 Peter 1:15). The public reading of the apostles' writings alongside those of the Old Testament further indicates that God was bringing together (and the church was accepting) the New Testament Scriptures as the Word of God. By the close of the first century the complete will of God had been revealed and recorded in the Scriptures.

Therefore we can dismiss the notion that the early church did not know the full extent of the New Testament canon until late into the fourth century, during which time the Catholic Church was the authoritative voice for the people of God. This line of reasoning gives the Catholic Church an authority that is reserved for the Scriptures alone.

### Scripture Is Sufficient

To justify its position, the Catholic Church often advances the argument that the Scriptures never claimed to be adequate to meet all our needs, based upon the words of the apostle John: "Jesus did many other things as well. If every one of them were written down, I suppose that even the whole world would not have room for the books that would be written" (John 21:25).

Read those words again and see if you think it was John's intention to state that the written Word of God, the inspired Scriptures, were never intended to be the only source of authority for our beliefs and practices. Did John really say that? John never even hinted at such a thought. In fact, he said the direct opposite.

In the previous chapter of his Gospel, John confirms that *what he tells us about Jesus is sufficient to secure for us eternal life.* When you have eternal life, you lack for nothing. *We find out how to have eternal life from the Scriptures.* This is what John says: "Jesus did many other miraculous signs in the presence of his disciples, which are not recorded in this book. But these are written that you may believe that Jesus is the Christ, the Son of God, and that by believing you may have life in his name" (John 20:30,31). As far as John is concerned, the written Word of God is adequate in meeting our needs. All we need to know about how to live, and how to die in the Lord, is contained in Scripture.

Remember that all of the Old Testament Scriptures which Jesus came to fulfill were canonized centuries before either Jesus came into the world or the Catholic Church came into existence. The procedure which God used to gather those books did not give the collecting agency an authority equal to that of the Scriptures. When God used the early church as his collecting agency in gathering together the books we know as the New Testament, he was not giving the church an authority equal to that of the Scriptures. *God gave us the Scriptures as our final and only authority in all matters of faith and morals.*

## FOR FURTHER READING

F.F. Bruce, *The Canon of Scripture* (Glasgow: Chapter House, 1988).

Norman Geisler and William Nix, *From God to Us* (Chicago: Moody Press, 1974).

J.I. Packer, *God Has Spoken* (London: Hodder and Stoughton, 1966).

# CHAPTER 3

# Which Is the One True Church?

*A* friend of mine had been speaking with a dear old lady whose comments caused him to wonder if they were speaking about the same thing. Finally, attempting to clarify the conversation, he asked her to define the Blessed Trinity. She confidently replied, "Faith, hope, and charity."

People also use the word church in a way that reveals confusion as to its true meaning. Here are just a few ex-examples:

"I believe in God but not in the church."

"I'm going to the church to say a few prayers."

"He never goes to church anymore."

"Our church is the finest building in town."

These statements reveal a lack of understanding of what the church is. We must return to the Scriptures to find our understanding of the church.

Let's begin with a look at Jesus' ministry.

### What Is the Church?

From the moment of his conception, Jesus' mission was tied to our spiritual recovery. An angel told Joseph the child that Mary was carrying was conceived by the Holy Spirit. The child was to be named Jesus "because he will save his people from their sins" (Matthew 1:21).

This redemptive theme was echoed by Jesus throughout his public ministry. He said he had come "to seek and to save what was lost" and "to give his life as a ransom for many" (Luke 19:10; Matthew 20:28). The mission of Jesus involved securing forgiveness of sins through the sacrifice of himself upon the cross.

"Didn't Jesus come to build his church?" you might ask (Matthew 16:18). Yes. Is the church, then, something in addition to Christ's redemptive mission? No. The Greek word for church is *ekklesia*, which literally means "called out." Jesus would build his church by calling people to be his disciples, forgiving their sins, and reconciling them to God and to each other by his death and resurrection.

When Scripture is compared with Scripture, a picture emerges of the church as a community of people whom Jesus has saved. For example, Paul says that Jesus bought the "church of God" "with his own blood" (Acts 20:28). John says that Jesus bought individuals with his blood: "... with your blood you purchased men for God from every tribe and language and people and nation" (Revelation 5:9). What then is the church? The church is *people whose sins have been forgiven*. The definition is as simple as that.

We can fine-tune our picture of the church by looking at the activities of Saul of Tarsus, later to become the great apostle Paul. Before his conversion to Jesus, Paul gave the church a rough time. In persecuting the church, Paul did not vandalize holy buildings. Instead, he persecuted holy *people*: "Saul began to destroy the church. Going from house to house, he dragged off men and women and put them in prison" (Acts 8:3). Later he recalled that those he persecuted were people who had come to believe in Jesus and had called upon the Lord for their salvation. This was the church that Paul had persecuted (Acts 22:4,19; Galatians 1:13).

Putting all this together, we see that the church does not include *all* people, not even all religious people. The church is specifically *those people whose sins have been forgiven*, whose faith rests in Jesus alone for salvation, people who have a new relationship with the Lord Jesus Christ. This is what Jesus came to bring into existence—a redeemed people. They are the true church of Christ.

## The Local Church

Through the preaching of the gospel, people were converted to the Lord Jesus Christ. In towns and cities these Christians formed local churches—congregations of God's people. This was certainly the apostolic practice: "For a whole year Barnabas and Saul met with the church and taught a great number of people. The disciples were called Christians first at Antioch" (Acts 11:26). Later Paul returned to some of the congregations he had helped establish and "appointed elders for them in each church" (Acts 14:23). When he finished his missionary journey, he and his companions "gathered the church together and reported all that God had done through them" (Acts 14:27).

A network of congregations was scattered throughout the known world. Though there is only one universal church over which Jesus is the head (Ephesians 1:21,22), the universal church is composed of thousands of local congregations. We read of "the churches of God" (1 Corinthians 11:16). Paul speaks of "the churches of Christ" (Romans 16:16). And those converted to the Lord in Thessalonica are simply referred to as "the church" (1 Thessalonians 1:1).

The size of these congregations varied, but in general they seem to have been small enough to meet in the homes of members (before purpose-built buildings made their appearance). Two outstanding servants of God were Priscilla and Aquila, whom Paul greeted along with "the church that meets at their house" (1 Corinthians 16:19). Greetings were also sent to "Nympha and the church in her house" (Colossians 4:15). Finally, when Peter was arrested, "the church was earnestly praying to God for him." Upon his miraculous release, "he went to the house of Mary the mother of John, also called Mark, where many people had gathered and were praying" (Acts 12:5,12).

There is one universal church, over which Jesus is the head. That church is composed of many local congregations scattered worldwide. People forgiven of their sins compose the church of God. That is the one true church revealed in the Bible.

### The Gospel of Love

Even a casual reading of the Bible tells us that love is a major Christian doctrine. Being raised as a Roman Catholic, I had been taught that God loved me, yet I had a very poor grasp of what God's love really meant. While God was very real to me, he was also very remote, and not very approachable. His love for me did not strike a responsive chord in my heart.

What contributed to my lack of understanding about God's love was my failure to see the connection between my sins and the death of Christ, which was the ultimate expression of the love of God. Yes, I believed I was a sinner and that Jesus died because he loved me, but what exactly did all this mean? These were religious terms that did not translate well into everyday understanding.

Like so many other Catholics, I had a sentimental view of the death of Jesus; I was moved to pity when I thought about him having to die such a cruel death. Yet there upon the cross God was exhibiting the depth of his love for all of us. To understand and appreciate that love we need first of all to know something about sin.

The Bible describes us as being lost, separated from God, and unable to save ourselves; ours is a hopeless condition indeed. But there is another dilemma which should leave us marveling at God's love and rejoicing at the announcement of such good news.

The dilemma that faced God was this: How could he forgive our sins and also see that justice was carried out? God could not simply forgive us and ignore the fact that we had broken his holy law, which carries a severe penalty.

Who would pay for our crime against God? We could not, for we stood self-condemned.

In Jesus Christ, the Father found One whose death would fully satisfy the demands of justice, thereby enabling him to forgive our sins. This is how the apostle Paul expresses the thought: "God presented him as a sacrifice of atonement through faith in his blood. He did this to demonstrate his justice, because in his forbearance he had left the sins committed beforehand unpunished—he did it to demonstrate his justice at the present time, so as to be just and the one who justifies those who have faith in Jesus" (Romans 3:25,26).

The cross of Christ vindicates God: It shows God to be just, in that he did what his own law demanded; he is also the one who justifies/pardons all those who have faith in Jesus. The love that God has for us can never be understood apart from a clear vision of the sacrifice of Christ.

God has never been short of sacrifices. Rivers of blood flowed from Israel's altars, yet they were unable to satisfy God's justice. Martyrs too numerous to mention gave their lives sacrificially in the service of the Lord, yet not even their death could satisfy God. Father Maximilian Kolbe, a Polish Franciscan priest, caught the attention of the world's press when his noble deed became known. He was a prisoner in Auschwitz concentration camp. When Kolbe heard that a married man with a family had been selected for execution, he volunteered to take this man's place. Kolbe became a substitute so that another man might live.

Jesus became our substitute when he took our sins upon himself: "He himself bore our sins in his body on the tree" (1 Peter 2:24).

The debt incurred by our sins could only be paid by an adequate sacrifice offered on our behalf. Though two other men died along with Jesus on that Good Friday, only *his* death was able to cancel our debt. Peter captures the concept of Christ being our substitute and Savior in these words: "Christ died for sins once for all, the righteous for the unrighteous, to bring you to God" (1 Peter 3:18).

## Sacrificial Power

The early Christians spoke in exclusive words about Jesus being the Savior of sinners, and they never entertained the idea that a person could be right with God apart from Christ. "Salvation is found in no one else," says Peter, "for there is no other name under heaven given to men by which we must be saved" (Acts 4:12). Paul is equally adamant when he says, "I resolved to know nothing while I was with you except Jesus Christ and him crucified" (1 Corinthians 2:2). Strange as it may seem, the cross of Christ displays neither weakness nor failure, but God's mighty power.

When I think of God's power, I think of some of the Lord's miracles. Power brings a dead man to life. Power restores the sight of one born blind or removes the dreaded disease of leprosy. Power calms a howling storm and then walks upon the water. To retrieve us from our lost condition and undo the damage brought by our sins demands nothing less than the power of God. "The message of the cross," Paul says, "is the power of God." He expresses the same truth by declaring, "I am not ashamed of the gospel, because it is the power of God for the salvation of everyone who believes" (1 Corinthians 1:18; Romans 1:16).

The gospel not only tells us that God forgives our sins, but it also tells us that there is no one whom God doesn't love. God's love is seen in sacrificial action. God did more than just talk about love. According to Paul, "God demonstrates his own love for us in this way: While we were still sinners, Christ died for us" (Romans 5:8). Though God was the offended party, he was the One who came in loving pursuit of each one of us, loving us unconditionally. He never asked that we show an interest in him and his ways before he would love us. He never demanded that we promise to turn over a new leaf and try a little harder. His love never laid down any conditions. That's the only reason any of us are in the church today, because Jesus loved us when we were outside the church. The love we now have for God springs from the fact that he first loved us (1 John 4:19).

The gospel speaks of God's unconditional love for us in sending us a Savior in Jesus Christ—a Savior whose death on the cross provided us with a way back to the Father. This is the gospel which Jesus commanded to be preached to all nations.

## The Obedience of Faith

Forgiveness is a free gift from God, and therefore cannot be earned by any deeds that we do. Neither is forgiveness a reward for achieving an acceptable standard of holiness. Both these views are common, though they are contrary to the teachings of Scripture.

Jesus pointed out the folly of trying to earn one's way to heaven when he told the parable of the Pharisee and the publican (Luke 18:9-14). The lesson was directed to "some who were confident of their own righteousness." Two men went up to the temple to pray. The Pharisee began his prayer by parading all of his good deeds before God. Pride filled his heart as he thanked God that he was not like those around him: robbers, evildoers, adulterers, or even the tax collector, whose profession was notorious for dishonesty. He continued his prayer with a reminder to God that he fasted twice each week and gave 10 percent of his income to the Lord.

The publican also prayed, but in a different tone. Jesus said that he stood at a distance and would not even raise his eyes to heaven, but in true repentance said, "God, have mercy on me, a sinner." Which of these two people was forgiven? It was the publican, Jesus said, and not the Pharisee that found favor with God. Why didn't the Pharisee find favor with God? After all, he believed in God, said his prayers, and lived a good life. Where did he go wrong? The problem with the Pharisee was that he was trusting in the *performance of his religious duties* to save him. The Pharisee didn't believe he was sinless, but felt that his good deeds, which were many, would tip the scales of God's justice in his favor. The good deeds of his life would more than compensate for his failings, and he would surely get a favorable verdict. So he thought.

The religious practice of the Pharisee reminds me of the time I saw two children playing on an escalator. They were trying to go up the stairs that were coming down. No matter how hard they tried, they failed; the stairs kept bringing them back to where they started. Finally they got off and went over to the stairs that were moving upward, stepped on, and let the stairs take them to the top.

## Not by Our Deeds

People are still trying to get to heaven under their own steam. They are trusting that their lives are good enough, that they have done their religious duties and have lived a pretty decent life overall. They entertain the idea that God will inspect their lives and, based on how they did while on earth, either let them into heaven or banish them for eternity.

Forgiveness is not obtained on the basis of our deeds, no matter how honorable they are. Forgiveness comes from God and we accept it by faith. As a Catholic I believed that my good deeds contributed toward my salvation; these included various acts of charity, participating in novenas, attendance at weekly Mass, frequent confession, and anything else that was my religious duty to perform. I understood loyalty to the Church as loyalty to God, and therefore all that the Church commanded I tried to obey. I believed that all my good deeds would count for something, producing a certain amount of credit that could be taken into account on the day of judgment.

An inescapable conclusion comes from such a line of thinking: If we are contributors to our own salvation, then we must say that the death of Jesus was not only inadequate but unnecessary. The apostle Paul put it this way: "If righteousness could be gained through the law, Christ died for nothing" (Galatians 2:21).

There are many wonderful Catholics who live their lives on a religious treadmill because of what they are taught about salvation. For years I was spiritually frustrated, weary of making new promises to God, only to fail yet again. I didn't know (because it was never taught, and still is not taught) that forgiveness is a free, unmerited gift from God, and that there is absolutely nothing we can do to earn it or deserve it. Furthermore, it is a gift that is not maintained by our deeds, either. Just as certain as we cannot save ourselves, we cannot keep ourselves saved. Jesus alone is the Savior.

Jesus came into the world to set us free, to give us new life, and not to supply us with a new set of rules and regulations to be obeyed in order to get to heaven. The last thing any of us needs is a religion that is based upon our performance; what we need is someone to give a perfect performance *for* us, and we find that performance accomplished in Jesus Christ. Listen to how clearly the Word of God speaks on this important subject: "It is by grace you have been saved, through faith—and this not from yourselves, it is a gift from God—not by works, so that no one can boast" (Ephesians 2:8,9).

Our response to God's offer of pardon cannot have any overtones of having earned or deserved the free gift of eternal life. For example, if you are sick and begin taking medicine; three times a day you pour the medicine into a spoon and drink it. Several days later you are fully recovered. What has made you well—the medicine or the spoon? The medicine, of course! You would never think of writing to the spoon manufacturer to thank them for your speedy recovery. Let me state it one more time: There is nothing we can do to save ourselves; we must simply "turn to God in repentance and have faith in our Lord Jesus" (Acts 20:21).

### True Repentance

Repentance is another word that has strayed far from its original meaning. Being sorry for sin and promising never to do it again is the standard understanding that most people have about repentance, but that meaning is quite different from what the Bible calls repentance. For example, a person can spend an evening consuming large quantities of alcohol. The next morning, with head throbbing and nerves jumping, he stumbles toward the medicine cabinet vowing, "Never again. I'll never touch another drop as long as I live." Though he may never take another drink, if he doesn't turn his life over to God, he has not truly repented. What he has expressed is deep remorse and regret, but that is not godly repentance.

It is very easy for Catholics to turn "repentance" into yet another good deed to be performed in order to obtain forgiveness. The danger is very subtle, but very real: We sin, we repent, we are now back in God's favor, and our repentance is credited with having achieved that result. Once repentance takes on the overtone of a savior, we tend to have faith in our repentance, in the performance of our religious duty. Unless that misunderstanding is corrected, a life on the religious treadmill follows quickly.

Repentance and turning to God are inseparably linked. When we repent, we make a conscious decision to turn away from sin because it offends God and to turn our life in God's direction; we determine to live in obedience to him. Godly repentance not only involves a change in our behavior, but also in our belief. We turn our life over to God. Scripture says, "Godly sorrow brings repentance that leads to salvation and leaves no regret, but worldly sorrow brings death" (2 Corinthians 7:10).

Zacchaeus was a wealthy tax collector who heard about Jesus' miracles and his claim to be the promised Messiah. Anxious to see Jesus, but prevented because of his small size, Zacchaeus climbed a sycamore tree in order to get a view of Jesus as he passed by. When Jesus saw him he called out, "'Zacchaeus, come down immediately. I must stay at your house today.' So he came down at once and welcomed him gladly."

Zacchaeus' encounter with Jesus moved his heart to repentance. "Here and now," he said, "I give half of my possessions to the poor, and if I have cheated anybody out of anything I will pay back four times the amount." That is godly repentance. Because of his penitent heart and obvious faith in Jesus, the Lord said to Zacchaeus, "Today salvation has come to this house" (Luke 19:1-10). Salvation comes to those who repent and have faith in Jesus. Without repentance there is no salvation.

The call to repentance is a recurring theme in the Scriptures. John the Baptist insisted that his disciples "produce fruit in keeping with repentance" (Matthew 3:8). John wanted the people not only to believe in Jesus the Messiah, but to demonstrate that they had turned their lives away from sin by displaying the evidence of true repentance. Jesus commanded that "repentance and forgiveness of sins . . . be preached in his name to all nations, beginning at Jerusalem" (Luke 24:47). Peter told his audience that they were to "repent and be baptized. . . ." Later he told others, "Repent, then, and turn to God" (Acts 2:38; 3:19).

Repentance must not be thought of only in negative terms: We stop committing sins. It is much more than that. The positive side of repentance is that we have decided to change the direction of our spiritual lives and to follow God. That is true godly repentance!

Because repentance involves turning to God, it is closely associated with faith. Paul said, "I have declared to both Jews and Greeks that they must turn to God in repentance and have faith in our Lord Jesus" (Acts 20:21).

## Real Faith in Jesus

Faith simply means to trust or believe. Abraham is the man whose faith is held up as the model for us today (Romans 4:16). Abraham's life was punctuated with demonstrations of his faith. God told him to leave his home and go to a foreign land. "By faith Abraham, when called to go to a place he would later receive as his inheritance, obeyed and went, even though he did not know where he was going" (Hebrews 11:8). That's faith!

God promised a son to Abraham. Time passed and the promise remained unfulfilled. Abraham was 99 years old and his wife, Sarah, was 90 when God spoke to him again about the promise of a son. Though surrounded by physical impossibilities, Abraham still had faith that what God had said would come to pass. "By faith Abraham, even though he was past age—and Sarah herself was barren—

was enabled to become a father because he considered him faithful who had made the promise" (Hebrews 11:11). That's faith!

When his son Isaac was grown, Abraham was commanded by God to offer him as a sacrifice. "By faith Abraham, when God tested him, offered Isaac as a sacrifice" (Hebrews 11:17). God never allowed Abraham to take the young man's life, though Abraham was prepared to do so, and for this reason Abraham is called "God's friend" (James 2:23). That's faith!

The type of faith that Abraham displayed in his life is the kind of faith that God wants us to have. When God tells us something, he wants us to believe it to be true and to respond accordingly. When he asks us to obey him, he expects obedience. Lip service is not what the Lord wants from us. Jesus asked a group of religious people, "Why do you call me 'Lord, Lord,' and do not do what I say?" (Luke 6:46). True faith will always do what God commands.

### Biblical Baptism

God has provided us with a Savior in Jesus Christ, who offers us the pardon of all our sins. That gift of forgiveness cannot be earned by anything we do. Our trust must be in the perfect sacrifice which Jesus offered to the Father for our sins. When Peter preached the gospel on the day of Pentecost, the Holy Spirit convicted thousands of listeners of their sinful condition and of their urgent need for pardon. They cried out to Peter and the other apostles, "Brothers, what shall we do?" Peter said to them, "Repent and be baptized, every one of you, in the name of Jesus Christ for the forgiveness of sins. And you will receive the gift of the Holy Spirit. . . . Those who accepted his message were baptized, and about three thousand were added to their number that day" (Acts 2:37,38,41).

Those who were baptized had faith in the sacrifice which Jesus offered to secure their forgiveness. They did not trust what they were doing, but trusted what Jesus had done for them. Their faith was not in a sacrament, but in a wonderful Savior. They trusted Christ crucified, not the Church, for their salvation. In their baptism they were identified by faith with Jesus in his death, burial, and resurrection (Romans 6:1-6).

From Pentecost onward the apostles proclaimed forgiveness of sins in the name of Jesus Christ. Those who believed that message were baptized in his name. We read that when the Samaritans "believed Philip as he preached the good news of the kingdom of God and the name of Jesus Christ, they were baptized, both men and women" (Acts 8:12).

When the gospel was preached to the first Gentiles and they came to believe in Jesus, Peter "ordered that they be baptized in the name of Jesus Christ" (Acts 10:48). When Paul taught the gospel, many believed and were "baptized into the name of the Lord Jesus" (Acts 19:5). What the apostles were doing was carrying out what Jesus had commanded: to go and make disciples of all people, and to baptize those who had come to believe in him (Matthew 28:18-20).

The same procedure is repeated again and again in the Bible. All the examples of people being baptized spoke of knowledgeable believers, not infants. As a Catholic, when I first read this fact in the Bible it was all new to me. Yet it doesn't take a degree in theology to know that when Jesus commanded the gospel to be preached and believers to be baptized, this excluded anyone who lacked knowledgeable faith. The teaching of Scripture is that baptism without faith in the sacrifice of Christ is a meaningless act, an empty ritual.

In baptism we are identified with Christ in his death, burial, and resurrection. We consciously make a break with the world and its ways and commit our life to one Lord for as long as we live. In many ways baptism is like marriage. A couple begins dating, and falls in love, and they plan to marry. In their wedding vows they commit themselves to each other for life. From that point onward they enter into a new relationship as husband and wife. Likewise baptism marks the beginning of a new relationship with the Lord.

To baptize means to dip or immerse in water. The practice of pouring or sprinkling water on the head of the one being baptized is a departure from the biblical command. Some might think this is just wrangling about words, but we are discussing words used by Jesus himself. When he said "baptize," he meant the accepted understanding of that word: immerse.

Just read the accounts of the Lord's baptism and that of the Ethiopian to see that baptism means an immersion in water. After Philip taught the Ethiopian, "...both Philip and the eunuch went down into the water and Philip baptized him. When they came up out of the water..." (Acts 8:38,39). The baptism of our Lord tells the same truth: "As soon as Jesus was baptized, he went up out of the water..." (Matthew 3:16). Obviously he had to have been in the water to come up out of it! We need to take our definition of baptism directly from what God has said in Scripture. Only then can we claim to be the one true church which Jesus came to establish.

## The Living Church

After Jesus ascended to heaven, he left the church to be his witness in the world. To ensure that the church in every generation would be mature in the faith, the risen Lord gave gifts to the church: evangelists, pastors, and teachers, whose ministry would be to build up the body of Christ for the work of service (Ephesians 4:11-16). The faithful teaching of the Scriptures to the people of God ensures that the church fulfills its God-ordained role to be the body of Christ in the world.

Conversion to Jesus is a supernatural occurrence, and we can expect to see a radical change in the lifestyle of those converted. Enjoying fellowship together was a prominent feature of the life of the early Christians. They met to receive instruction in the Word of God and to engage in prayer and praise to the Lord who had redeemed them from their sins (Acts 2:42-47). They gathered together each

Sunday to express thanks to their Savior and to remember his sacrifice as they held communion with him and with each other in partaking of the Lord's Supper (Acts 20:7; 1 Corinthians 11:17-34). Within their assembly, the needs of the members were met through the various gifts enjoyed by the church. Everyone had something to contribute to the overall well-being of the local church. As a result, the members were edified and refreshed by having been together (1 Corinthians 14:26).

The Lord can do great things with faithful people, and he is always looking for congregations he can depend on to carry out his will. One such congregation was in the city of Philadelphia. Jesus commended this church for their fidelity: "You have kept my word," he said, "and have not denied my name." Even though they were a people who had little strength and did not have a high profile in society, Jesus placed before them a great opportunity to serve him (Revelation 3:8). These insignificant people became the vehicle through which Jesus would be glorified.

Along with faithfulness to the Lord, the early church was marked by an extraordinary spirit of generosity. Christians began selling their property and sharing their possessions with those in need. The Scriptures tell us, "All the believers were together and had everything in common" (Acts 2:44). Even the poor shared out of their deep poverty in order to relieve the needs of those less fortunate than themselves. The explanation for their spirit of liberality is that "they gave themselves first to the Lord" (2 Corinthians 8:5).

Today's church must also be marked by that spirit of generosity and "not forget to do good and to share with others, for with such sacrifices God is pleased" (Hebrews 13:16). It is to the praise of God that generous people are still found in his church. These are people who continue to make big sacrifices for the sake of others. They are people who are prepared to lower their standard of living, miss a summer vacation, or cash in an insurance policy so that funds are available to meet the needs of others.

Thank God for the legions of men and women who give many hours of their time to teach children about God! These are the people who capture the true meaning of Jesus' words, "It is more blessed to give than to receive" (Acts 20:35). Their lives are a clear testimony that the church is alive and well and serving in this world.

## The Caring Church

The church must also be a caring community of people. There is a reason why the church is called the body of Christ and we its members. The apostle Paul argues that, just as the physical body is dependent on each member to enable the body to function correctly, so the church is dependent on its members to work as one body (1 Corinthians 12:15-26). A spirit of indifference has no place among God's people. The attitude that says "It's none of my business" is unacceptable because it is unlike Jesus' attitude. We are instructed in the Scriptures, "Remember the prisoners, as though in prison with them; and those who are ill-treated, since you yourselves also are in the body" (Hebrews 13:3 NASB).

Within the church there will be some who are strong and others who are weak and struggling. The battle of life is hard on the struggling, and they often grow discouraged and downhearted. We all know people who have had more than their share of tough breaks in life. Even for those with the strongest will in the world, continuous trials can wear them down. All of us in the body of Christ have an obligation to help such people. They are our wounded brothers and sisters, members of God's family, and we are to be their strength and hope—the arm they can lean upon, the shoulder they can cry on, and the ear that is open to hear their pain. If the church were only for the strong, few of us would make it.

What attracted the worst of sinners to Jesus was his kind and compassionate spirit. They had heard him often enough to know that they had found a true friend in Jesus. It didn't make any difference which side of the city they came from, and it didn't matter if their lives had been steeped in sin; he had time for them. Few of them moved in the "right" circles or had political clout that could influence the course of events. Jesus came to mend their broken lives, to restore their dignity, and to give them hope. Everyone was welcome.

The goal of every congregation of God's people must be to become imitators of their Lord and Savior, ministering to the needs of all and spreading the joyful news that this life is not all there is. There is life beyond the grave for the obedient because Jesus died and rose from the grave on the third day. Because Jesus lives, his church is a living body. This is the true church of the living Christ.

# CHAPTER 4

# Is the Papacy Taught in Scripture?

Since Vatican II the image of the Papacy has changed dramatically. The Papacy has been brought out of the Vatican to the people. It is now commonplace to see the Pontiff traveling throughout most of the world. In most countries a Papal visit is a national event, with audiences numbering in the millions. The Papacy has been given celebrity status by the media, and Papal messages are major news items. The strong stand taken by the Papacy in highlighting the evils of abortion and homosexuality is admired by many who have seen their own religious leaders grow soft and indifferent to these matters.

Who has not been impressed with the backdrop provided by St. Peter's and the Sistine Chapel for Papal coronations? The colorful uniforms of the Swiss Guards and the purple robes of the Princes of the Church add to the splendor of the occasion.

## What Does Scripture Say?

It would be easy to conclude that the Papacy must have a generous endowment of both scriptural and early historical evidence for its existence. However, the Papacy as we know it today has evolved over many centuries and bears no resemblance to anything we read about in the Scriptures. Not only is the Papacy a departure from what the Scriptures teach, but many of the doctrines pronounced with Papal approval are in contradiction to the written Word of God.

The Catholic Church would maintain that no such conflicts exist and that the Papacy has been given to the church by Jesus Christ. If this is so, then every serious-minded follower of Christ must accept this as being true. Hence there is a need to investigate the claim in the light of the Scriptures.

The Catholic Church maintains that the Papal office can be found in the words of Jesus spoken to the apostle Peter: "You are Peter, and on this rock I will build my church." There is no dispute that this is what the Lord said, but exactly what he meant must be arrived at by a careful study of this particular section of Scripture. The golden rule to follow when interpreting Scripture is to examine the text in the context in which it is found. By doing this we allow the text to reveal its own meaning rather than making the mistake of importing something into the text that is not really there. Let us read the entire section of Scripture we are about to examine:

> When Jesus came into the district of Caesarea Philippi, He began asking His disciples, saying, "Who do people say that the Son of man is?" And they said, "Some say John the Baptist; some, Elijah; but still others, Jeremiah, or one of the prophets." He said to them, "But who do you say that I am?" And Simon Peter answered and said, "Thou art the Christ, the Son of the living God." And Jesus answered and said to him, "Blessed are you, Simon Barjona, because flesh and blood did not reveal this to you, but My Father who is in heaven. And I also say to you that you are Peter, and upon this rock I will build My church; and the gates of Hades shall not overpower it. I will

give you the keys of the kingdom of heaven; and whatever you shall bind on earth shall be bound in heaven, and whatever you shall loose in earth shall be loosed in heaven" (Matthew 16:13-19 NASB).

## Upon This Rock

Controversy surrounded the identity of Jesus; opinions were in a constant state of flux. Some said he was an evil troublemaker, while others said he must be from God. Jesus was aware of what the opinion polls were saying when he asked his apostles who people thought he was. Their reply showed the extent of the speculation surrounding his identity.

Was he any of the above-mentioned characters, or was he someone else? Peter's confession that Jesus is the Christ, the Son of the living God, came by way of divine revelation from the Father and not by human speculation.

When Jesus spoke about building his church upon a rock, what was he referring to? In answering this question it is vital that we not lose sight of what the Father had just revealed about Jesus. When the Father endorsed Jesus as his Son, he was saying that Jesus is God the Son, equal in every way to God the Father (John 10:30-36). It does not make sense to think that Jesus would talk about building his church and, in the very same context, have nothing to say about the revelation the Father had just made known about Jesus' true identity.

When we think of building something, we think of the need for a foundation. If the building is to last, then the foundation must be solid. The church that Jesus came to build must also have a solid foundation. It will have to be a foundation which has been tested and found reliable, a foundation which can endure for all time, and one upon which all generations of Christians can confidently place their faith.

There is only one Person who qualifies to provide such a foundation—Jesus, the Christ, the Son of the living God. His deity is the solid rock, the unshakable foundation upon which the church rests. The writings of the apostles confirm that the church is indeed built upon Jesus, that he alone is the rock upon which the church is established (1 Peter 2:8; Ephesians 2:20; 1 Corinthians 3:11; 10:4).

## The Keys of the Kingdom

What then did Jesus mean when he gave Peter the "keys of the kingdom"? The most prominent statue in our local church was that of Saint Peter. He was an austere figure seated upon a throne, with one hand raised toward heaven and the other holding two large keys. I seldom passed that statue without being reminded of Jesus' words to Peter, "I will give you the keys of the kingdom of heaven." How are we to understand these words? By putting a number of questions to the problem we are trying to solve, we can arrive at the correct answer.

First, what are keys used for? Keys are used to allow us access to places previously closed. When Jesus gave Peter the keys of the kingdom of God, he gave him the means of opening the way into the kingdom of heaven.

Second, how did Peter use these keys to allow us access into the kingdom of heaven? Peter was the first to preach the gospel to both the Jews and Gentiles. Those who believed in Jesus were baptized in his name and entered the kingdom of heaven (Acts 2:38; 10:48). Of course, the other apostles were also engaged in this evangelistic work, but Peter did have a prominent role to play initially.

Keys were spoken about by Jesus on another occasion— the time he rebuked the religious leaders of his day for the way in which they abused the truth that God had revealed. The way they handled truth was a hindrance rather than a help to those who heard them. "Woe to you lawyers!" Jesus said. "For you have taken away the key of knowledge; you did not enter in yourselves, and those who were entering in you hindered" (Luke 11:52 NASB).

When Jesus spoke of the keys of the kingdom he symbolized the gospel, which opens the way back to the Father for all who will embrace its message.

## Binding and Loosing

After giving Peter the keys of the kingdom of heaven, Jesus delegated authority to him to carry out his ministry. "Whatever you shall bind on earth," Jesus said to Peter, "shall be bound in heaven, and whatever you shall loose on earth shall be loosed in heaven." This was not a blank check for Peter to do whatever he wanted. The authority to bind and loose was given in the context of preaching forgiveness of sins through the gospel. This harmonizes with the Lord's parting words to the apostles: "If you forgive the sins of any, their sins have been forgiven them; if you retain the sins of any, they have been retained" (John 20:23 NASB). Binding and loosing are equivalent to retaining and forgiving sins. How does this work out in practice?

On the Day of Pentecost, Peter preached the gospel and 3000 people believed that message and received remission of their sins (Acts 2:38-41). These people were loosed from their sins when they were forgiven. The sins of those who rejected the gospel were retained or bound. The authority to bind and loose was not exclusively Peter's, though he played a prominent role. All the apostles were engaged in opening the way to heaven through preaching the gospel, thereby binding and loosing the sins of the impenitent and the penitent. However, this does not exhaust the meaning of the Lord's words.

The authority to bind and loose was given by Jesus to every congregation of believers. Jesus made provision for the church to deal with problems that present themselves in the local congregation. He said that when an offender in the church refuses to repent of his wrongdoing, having first been confronted privately, then before witnesses, and finally before the church, the fellowship of the church is no longer to be extended to that person. He is to be rejected. What the church does on earth is what God has already done in heaven. That is what the Lord meant when he gave instruction not just to Peter, but to the whole church: "Truly I say to you, whatever you shall bind on earth shall be bound in heaven; and whatever you loose on earth shall be loosed in heaven" (Matthew 18:18).

Taken on their own, the words that Jesus spoke to Peter might seem to favor the view held by the Roman Catholic Church—that Peter alone was given supreme authority over the whole church. However, we have seen that the Scriptures show us a completely different picture. Peter was not given sole authority over the church; Jesus gave to every congregation of his people the authority to bind and loose the sins of the impenitent and the penitent. This teaching is enshrined in the Scriptures, which the Lord provided for the church to follow.

### Feed My Sheep

On the third occasion that Jesus appeared to his apostles after his resurrection, he probed into Peter's heart (John 21:1-17). Peter and his companions had gone fishing without much success. A lone figure on the shore called to them to let their nets down on the other side of the boat. They did, and their nets were filled with fish. Peter recognized that it was Jesus, and, throwing himself into the water, he swam ashore.

After eating, Jesus asked Peter if he loved him. Peter assured the Lord that he did. Jesus then told Peter to feed his sheep. A second time the Lord asked Peter if he loved him. This time the question was expressed more intently. With tones of annoyance in his voice Peter assured the Lord that he did love him. Again Jesus told him to feed his sheep. If Peter thought that the Lord had finished his inquiry, he was wrong. For the third time Peter was questioned about his love for the Lord and again he affirmed his love for the Lord. Once again Peter was instructed to feed the sheep.

What possible purpose did Jesus have for doing what he did? There is a very human side to this encounter. Peter cannot have been feeling too good about himself. His ego was shattered and his self-confidence was at a low ebb, knowing he had not long before denied the Lord three times. One denial might be understandable, since he was under pressure at the time, but three denials could not constitute a slip of the tongue.

Peter needed the Lord to know that he loved him, and Jesus afforded him that opportunity. Jesus wanted Peter to know that, while he knew that Peter had denied the Lord three times, he had also heard him confess his love for the Lord three times. With each confession of love, Jesus commissioned Peter to feed his sheep. Peter's reinstatement was now assured. I love this story because it tells me that the Lord has time for all of us who, on occasion, fail him miserably. Jesus is very patient in giving us another chance.

What is unacceptable is the interpretation placed on this event by the Catholic Church. It is an interpretation out of harmony with the divine authority of the Scriptures and lacks support from early church history. The Catholic Church maintains that Jesus here entrusted to Peter the role of Pope, who would teach the bishops and clergy, who would in turn teach the church. But Peter alone was never entrusted with the task of teaching the whole church. The words of Jesus forbid such a notion.

Jesus promised the apostles that upon his return to heaven he would send them the Holy Spirit. The Spirit would guide them into all the truth, teach them all things, and bring to their remembrance all that Jesus had said during his ministry (John 14:26; 16:13). This leaves no room for the idea that Peter was given supreme authority in teaching the church.

The apostle Paul was adamant in stating that his teachings were not given to him by any man, Peter included. What Paul taught was given to him by way of revelation from Jesus Christ. The successful ministry he conducted all over the Gentile world was independent of instruction from Peter (Galatians 1:11,12). In his letter to the Ephesian church Paul says that God's plan to save both the Jews and Gentiles in one body, the church, was a mystery that God made known by the Holy Spirit not just to Peter, but to all the apostles (Ephesians 3:4-6; 2:19-22). The exclusive claim made for Peter by the Catholic Church is simply not taught in the Scriptures.

## The True Head

Look at the management structure of a major company and see that it resembles a pyramid: There is the chairman at the top, then the board of directors, the managing directors, the heads of departments, all the way down to the person who makes the coffee. That's fine for a company, but the church which Jesus established is not structured along such lines.

We search in vain for the smallest hint of the Papacy in the Scriptures. It simply is not there. The apostles never believed that the church was structured like a pyramid, with Peter at the top. Instead, they portrayed the church as a flock of sheep overseen by Jesus their Shepherd, a kingdom loyal to its King (Jesus), a bride faithful to her husband (Jesus), and a body whose head is Jesus (John 10:16; Revelation 19:16; Revelation 21:2; Ephesians 1:22,23).

If Peter were made the head of the church, we would expect to find ample evidence to support this position. Two letters that Peter himself wrote do not support the claims that are made on his behalf. The extensive writings of Paul, 13 letters in total, and five letters by the beloved apostle John offer no evidence to support the Catholic teaching on this matter. The overall tone of Scripture never favors the concept of the Papacy.

This is not to say that the church has no leadership, for Christ, who established his church, continues to endow the church with gifts to sustain her in this world. But the various teaching gifts given to the church never take us outside the boundaries of what the Scriptures say (Ephesians 4:9-16).

## Changing History

In June 1989 the world news was dominated by events in China. Students took to the streets demanding a democratic society. But the hopes they entertained were short-lived, for troops and tanks moved in and indiscriminately massacred innocent people. Military courts tried and executed dozens of people whom Western reporters said were used as scapegoats. The international community was out-raged and registered a strong protest to the Chinese gov-ernment.

The official line fed to a nation of people that makes up a quarter of the world's population was that only a few people were killed, mainly soldiers. The events of June 1989 were being officially distorted. When people do not know their history they are liable to believe just about anything.

Most Catholics are not familiar with the history of their Church. I certainly wasn't. I knew the Church had some dark spots in its history, but otherwise the Church func-tioned like a well-oiled machine. For example, one could be forgiven for thinking that Papal infallibility has always been accepted by the Catholic Church. None of us can remember a time when it did not exist; we assume that it always existed. Even if it was not fully developed, it was there in embryo.

Not so!

## Changing Doctrines

Pope Pius IX defined the Immaculate Conception of Mary in an *ex cathedra* pronouncement on the eighteenth of December 1854. This was a new doctrine that ran contrary not only to the supreme authority of the Scriptures, but to a history of belief that denied that Mary was conceived with-out sin. A noted group of scholars and Church Fathers, including Pope Gregory the Great, are on record as oppos-ing such a belief. However, an infallible statement was made contradicting what another Pope had said.

Controversy continued to surround Pius IX. In 1870 he issued another *ex cathedra* pronouncement in which he defined Papal infallibility. Like the Immaculate Concep-tion, this new teaching had historical evidence stacked against it. Even the Catholic Church had been teaching that infallibility was not Roman Catholic teaching. While doing research on this subject some years ago, I obtained a copy of Keenan's Catechism published in 1860, from the Catholic

Library in Dublin. It shows clearly that infallibility was not believed among Roman Catholics:

> Q. Must not Catholics believe the Pope in himself to be infallible?
> A. This is a Protestant invention; it is no article of the Catholic faith; no decision of his can oblige, under pain of heresy, unless it be received and enforced by the teaching body; that is, by the bishops of the Church.[1]

In 1837 Bishop Purcell defended the teachings of the Roman Church in a public debate. His remarks about infallibility are pertinent, since they were made many years before infallibility was defined as Catholic faith:

> Appeals were lodged before the bishop of Rome, though he was not believed to be infallible. Neither is he now. No enlightened Catholic holds the Pope's infallibility to be an article of faith. I do not; and none of my brethren, that I know of, do. The Catholic believes the Pope, as a man, to be as liable to error as almost any other man in the universe. Man is man, and no man is infallible, either in doctrine or morals.[2]

Later Bishop Purcell changed his views. Upon returning from the Vatican Council in 1870 he preached a sermon in which he said, "I am here to proclaim my belief in the Infallibility of the Pope, in the words of the Holy Father defining the doctrine."[3]

It is extraordinary to see statements being made by Roman Catholic Bishops that say that no enlightened Catholic believes the Pope to be infallible and that infallibility is nothing other than a Protestant invention. Yet we hear that infallibility is now an official doctrine of the Church.

The majority of us who were reared as Catholics know very little about our history. We are led to believe that the doctrines of the Church can be faithfully traced back to the time of the apostles, and that over the centuries some of the doctrines that were present only in a small seed have been developed by the Church. It all sounds so reasonable. However, in the light of the facts presented from both the Scriptures and historical evidence, the Papal claim to authority over the church and his claim to infallibility must be rejected.

### An Unbroken Chain?

Is there an unbroken chain that can be traced from the present Pope all the way back to Peter? This has always been affirmed by the Catholic Church as being true; the Church claims that its bishops are successors to the apostles.

> Q. 16 What are the bishops of the Catholic Church?
>
> They are the successors to the apostles.[4]
> But in order to keep the gospel forever whole and alive within the Church, the apostles left bishops as their successors, "handing over their own teaching role" to them.[5]

Did you know that the apostles never actually appointed successors to take their place? Neither was there ever provision made by the Lord for the apostles to have successors. That must sound like a strange statement to people who have grown up being taught about apostolic succession. Reading the entire New Testament will not produce the slightest hint of apostolic succession. This was not an oversight on the part of the apostles. Quite the contrary.

Apostolic succession was impossible for the following reasons.

1. The apostles were eyewitnesses to the entire ministry of Jesus, having been with him from the beginning right up to his ascension to heaven. This made their ministry unique and unrepeatable. They could not appoint others to be successors to their own eyewitness experiences (John 15:27; Luke 24:48; Acts 1:8). When Matthias was chosen to

replace Judas, who had hanged himself, he had to have "accompanied us all the time that the Lord Jesus went in and out among us—beginning with the baptism of John, until the day that He was taken up from us—one of these should become a witness with us of His resurrection" (Acts 1:21,22 NASB). No one could possibly qualify on those terms today.

Though Paul was not among the original twelve, he was nevertheless an apostle. The miracles he performed were his apostolic credentials (2 Corinthians 12:12).

2. The apostolic ministry was unique in that it formed the foundation for the church not only in the first generation, but for all future generations (Ephesians 2:20). Once the foundation of the church was laid through the apostolic office there was no need for that office to continue in succeeding generations.

3. Through the apostles the full will of God was made known. Jesus promised he would send them the Holy Spirit to guide, teach, and recall to their minds all that he had said (John 14:26; 16:13). It was through the apostles that God's mystery of saving all people in one body, the church, was made known (Ephesians 3:4-6). The apostles were the channels through which all people would come to believe in the Lord Jesus Christ. To them Jesus gave the words the Father had given him (John 17:8). Looking toward the future, Jesus prayed "for those also who believe in Me through their word" (John 17:20 NASB).

Recognition of the unique office of the apostles paved the way for the church to accept their writings as canonical. Their writings were placed alongside those of the Old Testament prophets. The unbroken chain of true apostolic succession is found among those whose faith and practice have their roots in the apostolic faith. We don't have apostles today, but we do have their written word, inspired by God for our instruction (2 Timothy 3:16,17). To those who have an ear to hear, God's voice can still be heard in his living and abiding Word, the Scriptures.

## Nine Important Points

1. When Jesus called Peter, Peter left everything and followed the Lord. Catholics are incorrect to say that this included his wife. It didn't! Peter remained a married man throughout his apostolic life (Luke 4:38; 1 Corinthians 9:5).

2. Was Peter ever in Rome? There is absolutely no suggestion from the Scriptures that he was ever there. (Not that his presence there would prove anything conclusive.) When Paul wrote his epistle to the church at Rome he sent personal greetings to 27 people, but he never mentioned Peter (Romans 16:1-23).

3. The argument is sometimes made that Jesus gave Peter a special position by changing his name. No great significance can be placed on this argument, since Jesus also changed the names of some other apostles (Mark 3:16,17; cf. John 1:42).

4. When, in support of the primacy of Peter, the Catholic Church cites the lists of the apostles' names, Peter's name always appears first. However, when lists of the apostles' names in Scripture are compared, it can be seen that they are not identical in each Gospel account. This shows that the writers of the Gospels did not place any great significance on the order in which the names appeared (Matthew 10:2-4; Mark 3:16-19; Luke 6:13-16; Acts 1:13). The apostle Paul mentions Peter's name after having first mentioned the apostle John (Galatians 2:9).

5. Paul speaks about those who were regarded as "pillars" of the church. He names—in this order—James, Peter, and John (Galatians 2:9). What conclusion can be drawn from this? Paul's statement indicates that he never recognized Peter as having any standing in the church outside that of the other apostles. Peter was one of a number of leaders in the church, but certainly not the overarching leader.

6. The very fruitful ministry of the apostle Paul was conducted independently of Peter. Paul worked primarily with the Gentiles while Peter worked with the Jews. Over a period of 17 years Paul spent only 15 days in Peter's company. Yet Paul insists that the Lord who worked effectually

in Peter's ministry worked in the very same way in his own ministry. Everything the Lord was doing for Peter he was also doing for Paul. Both men were on equal footing in their respective ministries (Galatians 2:1,7-9). Yet Paul never claimed to be the Pope, and his statements show that neither did he recognize Peter as occupying the role which the Catholic Church has thrust upon him. None of the apostles did!

7. When all the lists of the various offices in the church are read, not once is the Papal office mentioned. If it existed, why is it omitted? Surely if the office were apostolic, we would have a record of it in the Bible! The reason for its omission is simple: The early church knew nothing of such an office (1 Corinthians 12:28-30; Ephesians 4:11-16).

8. When the early church met to resolve a problem that was upsetting the church, it was not Peter who made the final decision. In fact he was the fourth from last to speak, followed by Paul, Barnabas, and finally James, who drew the meeting to its final conclusion (Acts 15:6-23).

9. On one occasion the apostle Paul had to rebuke Peter to his face because he stood condemned by his own actions. Peter had withdrawn himself from Gentile Christians, thereby undermining the gospel. In plain terms Paul called Peter's behavior "hypocrisy" (Galatians 2:11-14). Peter was doctrinally wrong in what he did. Read the account in your Bible.

What conclusions can be drawn from the facts presented thus far? 1) The apostle Peter never recognized himself as being the Pope. 2) None of the other apostles recognized Peter as Pope. 3) There is not one mention of the Papacy in all of the Scriptures. 4) The emergence of the Papacy did not occur for several centuries after the church had been established. 5) "Infallible" statements have been seen to contradict the Scriptures.

There is only one sure road for each of us to travel, and that is the one laid out in the Scriptures. Everything in this world is changing; nothing is constant. Opinions change, doctrines change, views are modified, traditions are abandoned, and practices are updated, but God's Word remains firm, always trustworthy. Peter himself in one of his letters recalls for those early Christians, and for us, the permanence of the living and abiding Word of God: "All flesh is like grass, and all its glory like the flower of grass. The grass withers, and the flower falls off, but the word of the Lord abides forever. And this is the word which was preached to you" (1 Peter 1:24,25 NASB).

I cannot leave this chapter without answering a question that you as the reader might wish to ask me: Are you trying to reform the Catholic Church or are you calling people out of it? This is a fair question, leaving no room for sidestepping.

I don't believe that the Catholic Church as we know it will ever be reformed along biblical lines. The noble attempts of men like Luther prove that point. Jesus said that you do not put new wine into old wineskins, because old wineskins are brittle, and when new wine is poured into them, the wine ferments and the old wineskins cannot contain the new wine (Matthew 9:17). The point Jesus is making is this: The gospel that frees us from our sins cannot be contained within a legalistic religion.

Therefore those whom the Lord calls through the gospel of his Son see that they cannot remain in a Church whose fundamental message of salvation does not harmonize with the ancient message of Christ and his apostles.

However, my work is not to make people *anti-Catholic* but *pro-Christ*. He is the One who should receive all our attention.

# CHAPTER 5

# Did the First Christians Believe in the Mass?

Some of my earliest childhood memories have to do with going to Mass in a cold, drafty church. This was a duty I faithfully discharged.

The Mass was a minor spectacle for me in that there was something mysterious about what was happening on the altar. This is what religion is all about, I thought. The Mass was enhanced by the multicolored vestments worn by the priest, the decorated altar with its flowers and candles, and the proceedings uttered in the Latin tongue (at that time). If it was a high Mass, the smell of incense made the occasion all the more solemn. The incense hung in the air long after the priest had said *"Ite missa est"*—"Go, it is the dismissal."

I was taught that the Roman Catholic Mass was instituted by Jesus on Holy Thursday night, and that the Roman Catholic Church was the only faithful custodian of that night's proceedings. I thanked God I had not been born a Protestant.

## Shades of Belief

One of the difficulties I have in writing a chapter on the Mass is that it has various shades of belief. Most lay Catholics are familiar with the official teaching of the Church and tend to accept that doctrine, while many priests and theologians have views that do not square with official teaching.

I make this statement having spoken with priests, and also in the light of ongoing dialogue within various Christian traditions other than Roman Catholic. It is not unusual for Catholic theologians to be uncomfortable with the Church's teaching on the Mass, and to justify their reluctance to accept it on the grounds that a lot of new thinking is taking place on the subject. The only honest way I can deal with this subject is to present the doctrine from official Catholic sources.

> At the last Supper on the night which He was betrayed, our Savior instituted the Eucharistic Sacrifice of His Body and Blood. He did this in order to perpetuate the sacrifice of the Cross throughout the centuries until He should come again, and so to entrust to His beloved spouse, the Church, a memorial of His death and resurrection: a sacrament of love, a sign of unity, a bond of charity, a paschal banquet in which Christ is consumed, the mind is filled with grace, and a pledge of future glory is given to us.[1]

Isn't it strange how time has a way of changing us? I began in my mid-twenties reading the Bible, which for those of my generation was an entirely new experience. I found answers to my questions in the Bible, and I began to reflect on my religious heritage. I started to see the Mass in a different light. The Scriptures were bringing me back to the early church and its apostolic practice, providing the perfect starting place for examining the original meaning of Holy Communion.

## Early in Holy Week

The ministry of Jesus was coming to an end and hostility toward him was being mounted by the religious authorities. They sought opportunities to have him arrested and killed, not because they could prove anything against him, but because his teaching conflicted with the body of religious traditions they held sacred. In spite of their efforts, their plans to arrest Jesus had not materialized, and they must have wondered if those plans would ever be realized. Planning sessions were continued long into the night, and prayers for the arrest of this blasphemer were uttered from rabbinic lips. But the waiting was soon to end.

> "I'd like to speak to one of the chief priests. Tell him it is to his advantage that I speak to him immediately."
>
> "Who shall I say wishes to speak to him?"
>
> "My name is Judas; I'm one of Jesus' disciples."

Whatever planning session or prayer meeting was in progress at that time stopped, and the leaders gave their undivided attention to Judas. His desire to betray Jesus dovetailed perfectly with all that they had been planning and praying for. Scripture records their reaction: "They were delighted to hear this and promised to give him money" (Mark 14:11). They were delighted! Congratulations all around, for at last good fortune had come their way.

Such good fortune was seen as nothing other than divine intervention. Hadn't they prayed long and hard for this? And the evidence that God had answered their prayers was beyond dispute. Who would ever have thought that one of Jesus' own people would provide them with the opportunity of having him arrested? They all agreed that God does work in mysterious ways. How could they ever have doubted that God was on their side?

The next few days were important ones for Judas, who sought out the right moment to betray Jesus. He must be cautious and do nothing to arouse suspicion. After all, it's not every day of the week that one can earn 30 pieces of silver.

Unknown to his disciples, Jesus had made all the necessary plans to celebrate the Passover with them. They were to go to Jerusalem and follow a man carrying a pitcher of water. He would take them to an upper room which had been prepared for them. There they would celebrate the Passover together.

### The Passover

The Passover meal provided the setting for the institution of the Lord's Supper—Holy Communion. The common mistake has been to isolate the words of Jesus at the Lord's Supper from the historical context in which they were spoken, resulting in an understanding quite different from what Jesus originally intended. Many of us look back at our school days and rate history as one of the more boring subjects we had to study. However, it is to our advantage at this point to acquaint ourselves with the history of the Passover, and I will keep the historical review as brief as possible.

The first Passover occurred nearly 1500 years before Jesus was born. The descendants of Abraham had migrated to Egypt, and over the next 400 years grew from a few dozen people to nearly 3 million. The good relations which the Israelites had once enjoyed with the people of Egypt no longer existed, for now their numerical strength posed a threat to Egypt. To counter any possible rebellion, the children of Israel were subjected to slavery and cruelty.

However, God had not grown deaf to their cries, or forgetful of his promise to Abraham; his descendants would eventually live in a land flowing with milk and honey, the Promised Land. God raised up Moses to lead the people to freedom. God's repeated call to Pharaoh, "Let my people go," failed to move his impenitent heart. Verbal persuasion now gave way to a series of plagues, each plague being more severe than the one previous. The tenth and final plague was the death of every firstborn in each family, including the firstborn of the beasts in the fields. But no firstborn Israelite would be harmed by this plague if God's protective instructions were followed:

Go and take for yourselves lambs according to
your families, and slay the Passover lamb. And
you shall take a bunch of hyssop and dip it in the
blood which is in the basin, and apply some of
the blood that is in the basin to the lintel and the
two doorposts; and none of you shall go outside
the door of his house until morning. For the Lord
will pass through to smite the Egyptians; and
when He sees the blood on the lintel and on the
two doorposts, the Lord will pass over the door
and will not allow the destroyer to come in to
your houses to smite you (Exodus 12:21-23 NASB).

Israel did as God instructed. Each family killed a lamb,
and they were protected from God's judgment by sprinkling the blood of the lamb on their homes. Israel waited to
see what God would do:

It came about at midnight that the Lord struck
all the firstborn in the land of Egypt, from the
firstborn of Pharaoh who sat on his throne to the
firstborn of the captive who was in the dungeon,
and all the firstborn of cattle (Exodus 12:29 NASB).

That night Pharaoh summoned Moses and ordered him
to take the children of Israel out of Egypt. This deliverance
would be commemorated each year by succeeding generations of Israelites in their observance of the Passover.

This day will be a memorial to you, and you
shall celebrate it as a feast to the Lord; throughout
your generations you are to celebrate it as a permanent ordinance. . . . And it will come about
when you enter the land which the Lord will give
you, as He has promised, that you shall observe
this rite. And it will come about when your children will say to you, "What does this rite mean to
you?" that you shall say, "It is a Passover sacrifice
to the Lord who passed over the houses of the

sons of Israel in Egypt when he smote the Egyptians, but spared our homes" (Exodus 12:14,25-27
NASB).

Even the food which the Israelites ate at the Passover had
significance: The slain lamb recalled how God's judgment
was diverted by the lamb's blood; the bitter herbs spoke of
their unpleasant sojourn in Egypt; the unleavened bread
was called the bread of affliction (Deuteronomy 16:3).

This was the meal that Jesus celebrated with his disciples
in the upper room shortly before his death. This is the
context in which the words spoken by Jesus at the institution of the Lord's Supper must be examined.

### The Lord's Supper

The occasion was a solemn one; the conversation that
evening centered on God's deliverance of the children of
Israel from bondage in Egypt, and their eventual occupa-
tion of the Promised Land. Extracts from the writings of
Moses, who recorded the Exodus, would have been recalled or recited from memory. Freedom from bondage was
the recurring theme.

Jesus had often spoken of his own death in the context of
our spiritual liberation, a point that was not always understood by his apostles. Jesus used unleavened bread and
fruit of the vine from the Passover meal to speak of another
deliverance. This time the deliverance would not be from
the bondage of Egypt, but deliverance from the bondage of
our sins. This freedom would be secured not by our slaying
a lamb and sprinkling its blood upon our homes, as the
Israelites had done in Egypt centuries previously, but by
God providing his Son as the Lamb whose death would
take away our sins (John 1:29; 1 Corinthians 5:7).

> While they were eating, He took some bread,
> and after a blessing He broke it, and gave it to
> them, and said, "Take it; this is My body." And
> when He had taken a cup and given thanks, He
> gave it to them; and they all drank from it. And

He said to them, "This is My blood of the covenant, which is poured out for many. Truly I say to
you, I shall never again drink of the fruit of the
vine until that day when I drink it new in the
kingdom of God" (Mark 14:22-25 NASB).

As succeeding generations of Israelites commemorated
their freedom by observing the Passover meal, so Christians in succeeding generations would recall their spiritual
freedom by commemorating the death of Jesus in the
Lord's Supper. The Passover meal looked back to a point in
history when God set his people free. In the same way, the
bread and wine in the Lord's Supper look back to Good
Friday, when Jesus, our Passover Lamb, shed his blood and
offered himself as a sacrifice to set us free.

### The Sacrifice of the Mass

I recall my school days, and how each day began with a
half-hour of religious instruction. We were taught from a
little red book called *A Catechism of Christian Doctrine*. To its
credit, at least the book spoke in a clear, unambiguous
voice in answering the questions it posed. I can still recall
the answer to the question "What is the Mass?"

The Holy Mass is one and the same sacrifice
with that of the Cross, inasmuch as Christ, who
offered Himself, a bleeding victim, on the Cross
to His Heavenly Father, continues to offer Himself in an unbloody manner on the altar, through
the ministry of His priests.[2]

The teachings of the Council of Trent (1545-1564), which
are still binding today, leave no room for any misunderstanding:

If anyone says that in the mass a true and real
sacrifice is not offered to God . . . let him be
anathema (Canon 1).
If anyone says that by those words "Do this for
a commemoration of me," Christ did not institute the Apostles priests, or did not ordain that

they and other priests should offer his own body and blood, let him be anathema (Canon 2).

If anyone says that the sacrifice of the mass is one only of praise and thanksgiving; or that it is a mere commemoration of the sacrifice consummated on the cross but not a propitiatory one, let him be anathema (Canon 3).[3]

If the tone of the Council seems a trifle strong to our spirit of tolerance today, note two recent Papal encyclicals which reflect the teaching of the Council of Trent:

Pius XI in *Ad Catholici Sacerdotii* (1935) described the mass as being in itself "a real sacrifice... which has a real efficacy." Moreover, "the ineffable greatness of the human priest stands forth in its splendour," because he "has power over the very body of Jesus Christ." He first "makes it present upon our altars" and next "in the name of Christ himself he offers it a victim infinitely pleasing to the Divine majesty" (pp. 8-9). In *Mediator Dei* (1947) Pius XII affirmed that the eucharistic sacrifice "represents," "re-enacts," "re-news," and "shows forth" the sacrifice of the cross. At the same time he described it as being itself "truly and properly the offering of a sacrifice" (para. 72), and said that "on our altars he [Christ] offers himself daily for our redemption" (para. 77).[4]

The Papal encyclicals are official statements by the Catholic Church, and are said to reflect the will of God; they are too important to be pushed to one side and neglected. They must be examined in the light of what the Bible teaches. We owe it to ourselves to be pursuers of truth, and no safer ground can be occupied than placing our faith firmly in the teachings of Scripture. Let us now examine the Papal statements.

## Three Questions

First, is the Mass a real sacrifice that is offered daily? The Catholic Church says it is. "On our altars," Pope Pius said, "Christ offers himself daily for our redemption." In contrast to this pronouncement, the Scriptures teach that the sacrifice of Jesus is a onetime offering, occurring only as often as the death of man occurs—namely, once! (Hebrews 7:26-28).

Second, is the Mass a propitiatory sacrifice? The Catholic Church says that it is. The word "propitiation" means "satisfaction" and refers to the sacrifice of Jesus satisfying the divine justice of God. The proof that the Father accepted the one sacrifice of Jesus is seen in that the Father raised him from the dead and seated him at his own right hand. Now that our sins have been forgiven by the one sacrifice of Jesus, what purpose would a continual sacrifice serve? Once the ransom is paid and the hostages freed, the ransom does not have to be continually paid.

The consequence of believing that the sacrifice of Christ is a continuous offering is devastating because it undermines what Jesus' death achieved on Good Friday. We cannot believe that Jesus secured our full pardon by the sacrifice of himself and also believe that the Mass is a continual offering of that same sacrifice. The two views contradict each other.

This brings us to our final point: Did Christ institute the Catholic priesthood? The Catholic Church says that he did, and places an anathema (a curse) on those who deny this (Canon 2). Yet what purpose would such a priesthood serve? Let me stress again what Scripture says: With the forgiveness of our sins having been achieved by the one sacrifice of Christ, there is no need for that sacrifice to continue, and therefore no need for a priesthood as defined by the Catholic Church.

Whenever I have occasion to go to Mass for a wedding or funeral, I see how closely the Mass resembles the sacrificial service in the Old Testament. People in those days lived in the shadows, waiting for the future time when one priest would offer one perfect sacrifice for all time. Because the Catholic Church does not hold to this biblical truth, it has adopted the practice of holding Masses for almost every occasion.

Masses are offered for the living, the dead, the sick, and the dying. A Mass can be said for one's special intentions, wedding anniversary, or success in school exams. This practice is far adrift from what Jesus instituted. The simple commemorative meal has taken on a complexion that would not be recognized by the apostles.

Imagine the apostle Peter and his wife (he was married—Luke 4:38; 1 Corinthians 9:5) celebrating their wedding anniversary by having a Passover meal, or the family of Stephen, the first martyr, having a Passover meal at his funeral. What is the problem with that practice? The problem is that the Passover would be used outside its original purpose, since it actually has nothing to do with wedding anniversaries, funerals, etc.—and neither has the Lord's Supper.

## One Sacrifice

Offering animal sacrifices is not something we can identify with today; it all seems quite purposeless. Yet the offering of sacrifices figured prominently in the Jews' religious life. These sacrifices served as shadows announcing the coming of something real. They pointed to Good Friday, when one special Priest would offer one sacrifice that would achieve our forgiveness forever. This is what Jesus was referring to in the upper room when he spoke of shedding his blood for the forgiveness of our sins. He is the real sacrifice that came to fulfill all that had been foreshadowed. And the sufficiency of his one sacrifice is contrasted with the ineffective daily sacrifices offered by Israel's priests.

> Every priest stands daily ministering and offering time after time the same sacrifices, which can never take away sins; but He, having offered one sacrifice for sins for all time, sat

> down at the right hand of God.... For by one
> offering he has perfected for all time those who
> are sanctified.... Now where there is forgive-
> ness of these things, there is no longer any
> offering for sin (Hebrews 10:11,12,14,18 NASB).

The Scriptures make it clear that the sacrifice of Jesus was
a one time, unrepeatable sacrifice. His death is like his
resurrection—unrepeatable. I remember the first time I read
the Hebrew epistle and how greatly impressed I was with
its theme of Christ's superiority. Not only did Jesus bring a
superior covenant and possess a superior priesthood, but
his one sacrifice was superior to any other sacrifice that
ever has been or ever will be made again. I could no longer
reconcile the teaching of the Catholic Church (that the Mass
is a continuous sacrifice) with what I was reading in the
Word of God.

### The Apostles' View

The apostles were assembled with Jesus in the upper
room on the night he instituted the Supper. They heard the
words he used and saw exactly what he did. What was
their understanding of Jesus' words?

> While they were eating, Jesus took bread, and
> gave thanks and broke it, and gave it to his dis-
> ciples, saying, "Take and eat; this is my body."
> Then he took the cup, gave thanks and offered it
> to them, saying, "Drink from it, all of you. This is
> my blood of the covenant, which is poured out
> for many for the forgiveness of sins. I tell you, I
> will not drink of this fruit of the vine from now on
> until that day when I drink it anew with you in
> my Father's kingdom" (Matthew 26:26-29).

First, when Jesus took the bread and wine, and said it
was his broken body and shed blood, they knew he was not
to be understood literally. They could see Jesus standing
there in their presence, not yet having died! Furthermore,

they heard him say, after they had drunk the wine, "I shall never again drink of the fruit of the vine until that day when I drink it new with you in the kingdom of God." They had not drunk his literal blood, but the fruit of the vine.

Second, the apostles were Jews who held to strict dietary laws—laws that prohibited the eating of unclean foods or anything that contained blood (Acts 15:28,29). Do you think they would have eaten the literal flesh and blood of Christ? Years after the church had been established Peter said to the Lord, "I have never eaten anything unholy and unclean" (Acts 10:14 NASB). Peter could never have made that statement if he had in fact been eating and drinking the literal body and blood of the Lord.

Third, the apostles heard Jesus say that the Supper was to be a memorial of his death. The word "memorial" was familiar to them. It was used every time they celebrated the Passover, which pointed back to when God set his people free from slavery. The bread and wine would also be a memorial of Christ setting his people free from the bondage of sin. Let me clarify the point by way of an illustration.

Every nation has its own flag. When a head of state visits a country he shows his respect by saluting its flag. The flag represents that nation. Have we not all seen news reports of protesters burning another nation's flag? They are doing more than just burning a piece of colored material; they are displaying their opposition by burning what represents the country—namely, its flag. In the very same way, the bread and wine represent the broken body and shed blood of our Lord Jesus Christ.

Fourth, Jesus promised that his presence would be with his church for all time. Though he would return to heaven, through the Holy Spirit the real presence of Christ would reside, not in bread and wine, but in the Holy Spirit whom Jesus sent to be his divine replacement.

> I will ask the Father, and He will give you another Helper, that He may be with you forever; that is the Spirit of truth, whom the world cannot receive, because it does not behold Him or know

Him, but you know Him because He abides with
you, and will be in you. I will not leave you as
orphans; I will come to you (John 14:16-18 NASB).

Christ's presence is not in holy buildings, but in the lives
of his holy people. The Lord's presence resides in a new
tabernacle, a new temple which he has built—the church,
the saved people of God. This temple is not made of bricks
and mortar, but is composed of all Christians who are
called "living stones" in the temple of God (1 Peter 2:5-9).
Paul echoes the same thought when he says that all God's
people are "being fitted together" and are "being built
together into a dwelling of God in the Spirit" (Ephesians
2:19-22 NASB). This is the real presence of Christ.

Fifth, the apostles did not believe that Jesus performed a
miracle at the Supper by turning the bread and wine into
his literal body and blood. They did not believe in the
Catholic doctrine of transubstantiation, because no evidence of a miracle was present.

When Jesus turned the water into wine at the marriage
feast in Cana of Galilee, that miracle could be verified by
the senses; it looked like wine, it smelled like wine, and it
tasted like wine. There was no doubt about it: It was wine.
And those present at the wedding agreed that it was wine.
The miracle caused people to honor and glorify the Lord
(John 2:1-11). When Jesus cleansed the lepers, the change
in their appearance was obvious to everyone. No one
doubted that a miracle had occurred, least of all the lepers
(Luke 17:11-19). Yet no such evidence of a miracle exists in
transubstantiation.

### The Flesh and the Blood

The Bible clearly teaches that the Lord's Supper is a
memorial of Jesus' death and not a literal sacrifice. We have
seen that Christ is present, not in bread and wine, but in his
people through the Holy Spirit. He tabernacles (dwells) not
in holy places, but in a holy people, his church. This understanding paves the way for us to examine the Lord's words
in John chapter 6. Catholics have seen in the Lord's words in

John chapter 6 a reference to the Mass. But a careful study of the entire chapter shows that Jesus was referring to his death—the giving of his flesh and the shedding of his blood—to secure eternal life for us. Our faith must be in Jesus' death if we are to have eternal life.

Here is the background.

With five loaves and two fishes Jesus fed the multitudes that had been following him (John 6:1-14). The people responded by wanting to take him and make him their king, but Jesus declined (verse 15). The next day the people pursued Jesus to Capernaum, but their motives were impure; they wanted Jesus the miracle-worker, but not Jesus as the Lord of their life (verse 26). So Jesus spoke to them of the true bread that imparts eternal life (verse 27). Unlike the bread which Moses fed their ancestors in the wilderness, Jesus is the true bread come from heaven to impart eternal life (verses 30-59).

In mentioning eternal life Jesus introduced the necessity of his death. He would offer his flesh and shed his blood to secure eternal life for us. Speaking figuratively, Jesus said that one must "eat his flesh and drink his blood" to have eternal life (verses 52-56). Some of the hearers took offense at this, and turned from following him. They were offended because they thought Jesus was speaking literally when he spoke of having to eat his flesh and drink his blood. He wasn't! There was no purpose in calling these people back, for Jesus knew those who would not believe in him. The group who departed were not honest seekers, but unbelievers (verses 36,64).

Noting their departure and their misunderstanding of his words, Jesus said to those who remained, "The flesh counts for nothing" (verse 63). What flesh was Jesus speaking about? It was the *literal* flesh some had thought he was referring to: "How can this man give us his flesh to eat?" (verse 52). The previous day they had seen him literally distribute bread among them; would he now begin to literally distribute himself among them for eating? No, this is not what Jesus was talking about, and he confirms this fact by saying that the literal eating of his flesh will not impart eternal life: "It is the Spirit who gives life; the flesh profits nothing" (NASB).

How do we eat and drink the flesh and blood of Jesus so that we may have eternal life? The answer to the question is repeated several times in this chapter: *We eat and drink by coming to him in faith and believing in him.* That is what Jesus himself said:

> I am the bread of life. He who comes to me will never go hungry, and he who believes in me will never be thirsty (verse 35).

> Everyone who looks to the Son and believes in him shall have eternal life (verse 40).

> He who believes has everlasting life (verse 47).

Our Lord's discussion on the bread of life has no reference to the institution of the Lord's Supper. The whole thrust of Jesus' teaching is that we must accept, by faith, the flesh and blood he offered in the one sacrifice of himself to the Father for our eternal life.

## The Real Communion

If Holy Communion is not a continuous sacrifice, or the literal eating of the flesh of God the Son, then what is Holy Communion? The most informative passage of Scripture about the Lord's Supper/Holy Communion was written to the church in Corinth. The apostle Paul had come to that part of Greece and preached the gospel. Those who believed the claims of Jesus were baptized (Acts 18:8).

The membership of the church included people who came from pagan backgrounds (1 Corinthians 6:9-11). Some continued to display traits of their former religious practices, and this was having a devastating effect on their communion with the Lord. They were continuing to offer sacrifices to idols, which prompted Paul to give some apostolic instruction.

When you offer a sacrifice to an idol, Paul says, you are having fellowship or communion with the one who is responsible for that idol's existence—in this case, demons. Since you now belong to Christ, you cannot continue this practice and expect your communion with the Lord in his Supper to be holy. "You cannot drink the cup of the Lord and the cup of demons too; you cannot have a part in both the Lord's table and the table of demons" (1 Corinthians 10:21,22).

Furthermore, the Corinthians' unchristian treatment of each other when they came together as a church made their communion unholy (1 Corinthians 11:17-34). They gathered as a congregation of God's people to remember the most loving act this world has ever known, but all they could do was display a factious spirit among themselves. Though they ate the bread and drank the wine, their communion was nevertheless unholy. What made it unholy? Their unholy lives!

The Catholic teaching on Holy Communion is very different from what the Bible says. As a Catholic, when I went to Mass, I would go up to the altar to receive Holy Communion from the priest. Holy Communion was something one received, something material. Yet that is not what the Bible teaches.

Jesus intended that his church be one, where members of his body display the same care one for another, and where the spirit of Christ is seen in the lives of his people. When the local church comes together as the people of God, we are making a statement when we partake of the bread and wine; we are saying that Jesus our High Priest offered one perfect sacrifice to the Father on our behalf. And though we are many members we compose only one body, over which Jesus is the head. We are brothers and sisters in Christ and belong to one family with God as our Father. As a spiritual family we gather around the table of the Lord to commemorate the price Jesus paid to set us free from our sins. This is the memorial meal for the family of God as we wait for the Lord's return.

# CHAPTER 6

# *Should We Go to Confession?*

*I* remember making my first confession. For months our school class received instruction about confession in preparation for making our first Holy Communion. We were assured by the priest that there was nothing to be afraid of; it would be a wonderful experience. At the age of seven our class formed two lines and marched from school to the parish church. I entered the confession box with a mental list of all my sins.

"Bless me, Father, for I have sinned. This is my first confession."

With the priest's reassuring words I began my confession. I confessed that I often talked in church, looked around during Mass, and fought with my sisters—and that sometimes my mother said I wasn't good. I then promised I was going to change.

"You have made a very good confession," the priest said. "For your penance, say three Hail Marys."

This was the first of many confessions I made every week. As I grew older and my offenses moved from social misdemeanors to mortal sins, the occasion and frequency of those sins had to be recalled at each confession: I committed this sin eight times, that sin twice, and the other sin 18 times.

Confession made me feel better, but had little effect on my sinful behavior. The practice of confession continually reinforced in my mind the idea that the Church held the keys that could unlock the way of heaven for me, and that without the Church and its sacraments all that awaited me after death was an eternity in hell. Teachings like that had a way of getting my attention, especially when they were supported with horrific tales of the torments of hell. How could I ever doubt that I needed the Church? It was my lifeline to heaven.

**The Catholic Claim**

Going to confession is not something that many Catholics enjoy, and it is a source of fascination to those who are not Catholics. Just what goes on in the dark confession box? Confession is one of the seven sacraments of the Catholic Church, and the words of Jesus to his apostles provide the Church's proof text for this sacrament's existence:

> "Peace be with you; as the Father has sent Me, I also send you." And when He had said this, He breathed on them, and said to them, "Receive the Holy Spirit. If you forgive the sins of any, their sins have been forgiven them; if you retain the sins of any, they have been retained" (John 20:21-23 NASB).

Roman Catholics stand alone in their understanding of these words of Jesus, while those in other Christian traditions, who accept the Bible as their only authority, have traveled the path of the apostles and the practice of the early church. Irrespective of what religious label we wear, we are bound together by a common problem: We are sinners in need of pardon from a gracious, loving God whom we have offended. Since Jesus is the One who alone can forgive us, we need to examine his words to see how in fact we are forgiven.

On December 2, 1973, Pope Paul VI authorized the publication of *Rite of Penance*, which states:

> Our Savior, Jesus Christ, when he gave to his Apostles and their successors power to forgive sins, instituted in his Church the sacrament of penance. Thus the faithful who fall into sin after baptism may be reconciled with God and renewed in grace.[1]

> Moreover, the teaching of Trent and of the Church today is that "absolution is given by a priest, who acts as judge."[2]

> The Church teaches that it is necessary by divine law to confess to a priest each and every mortal sin—and also circumstances which make a sin a more serious kind of mortal sin—that one can remember after a careful examination of conscience.[3]

These statements show the unique claim being made by the Catholic Church that it has been entrusted by Christ with the power to forgive and retain sins through the sacrament of penance.

Is the Catholic practice of confession found in the Scriptures or in the life of the early church? How did the apostles forgive and retain sin? These are important questions that demand accurate answers. To avoid the danger of taking shortcuts, we must start with the announcement of a coming Savior who brings forgiveness of sins, and finally move to his subsequent charge to the apostles to forgive and retain sins. I will therefore deal with two aspects of forgiveness: 1) how our sins are forgiven initially and 2) how we are forgiven of sins committed after our conversion to Christ.

### The Good News of Forgiveness

Mary and Joseph were told that the child that Mary was carrying was the Son of God. He was coming into the world to "save His people from their sins" (Matthew 1:21 NASB). This theme of forgiveness was one that Jesus repeated throughout his ministry. "I have come," he said, "to seek and to save what was lost" and "to give my life as a ransom for many" (Luke 19:10; Matthew 20:28). The apostle John, in his epistle, echoes the reason why Jesus came: God sent his Son "that we might live through Him . . . to be the propitiation for our sins . . . to be the Savior of the world" (1 John 4:9,10,14 NASB).

We need a Savior because in our own spiritual condition we are sheep that have wandered far from God. Because we were unable to find our way home, Jesus the Good Shepherd came seeking us. He demonstrated that he is able to meet our need of forgiveness.

One day crowds came to the house where Jesus resided, filling it to overflowing. A paralytic man, brought by his friends, was unable to gain access to the Lord. Undaunted, his friends climbed onto the roof and made an opening through which they lowered the paralytic into the Lord's presence. Amazed by their display of faith, Jesus said to the paralytic man, "My son, your sins are forgiven." Horrified at what Jesus had said, the religious leaders exclaimed, "He is blaspheming; who can forgive sins but God alone?"

Knowing their thoughts, Jesus proceeded to take them out of their state of shock. "Which is easier," he asked, "to tell this man that his sins have been forgiven, or to enable him to walk?" No theological training was required to answer that question. To show that he had authority to forgive sins, Jesus told the paralytic man to "rise, take up your pallet and go home." Immediately the man, having been restored to perfect health, arose and walked out. The wide-eyed leaders exclaimed, "We have never seen anything like this" (Mark 2:1-12 NASB). The miracle demonstrated that Jesus had authority to forgive sins. He had come to forgive all who would confess their sins.

### Drama in the Temple

I read a true story that shows what forgiveness and reconciliation are all about. It involves a father whose son had been murdered by another youth. The father was a Christian and took his relationship with the Lord seriously. Instead of harboring hatred and bitterness in his heart, he imitated the Lord Jesus, whom he served.

He went to the prison and met the youth who murdered his son. He assured him that he and his family had forgiven him for the crime committed against them, though the pain suffered by the loss of his son would always be there. Through his repeated visits to the prison a relationship grew between them. The Christlike manner of the father eventually led the young man to a living faith in Jesus Christ. The criminal became the father's brother in Christ, and upon his release the father took him into his home and since then has treated him like his own son.

All of us need assurance that when we confess our sins God will in fact forgive us—and not just forgive us, but welcome us into his presence as his children. Jesus provided that assurance in a very dramatic fashion. When he died, the veil in the temple was torn from top to bottom (Matthew 27:50,51). The significance of what happened may be lost on those who are not familiar with the Old Testament, so a very brief visit to that part of God's Word is in order.

Adam and Eve lost paradise when they sinned. God drove them from the Garden of Eden, broke fellowship with them, and sent cherubim to guard the way back to the tree of life (Genesis 3:22-24). Many years later God instructed Israel to build a temple and to weave cherubim into the curtain/veil that separated the holy place from the holy of holies, where the presence of God resided (Exodus 36:35). Whenever an Israelite entered the temple he saw the veil with the cherubim and was reminded that sin separated man from God. That separation was soon to end.

When Jesus died, the veil in the temple was ripped apart from top to bottom. God was showing that access into his very presence was now possible because the death of Jesus had secured forgiveness of sins. Like the prodigal son, we too can come home to the Father. This was the message of forgiveness that Jesus told the apostles to proclaim to all nations. As he had been sent by the Father to achieve forgiveness, so also he sent the disciples to proclaim that forgiveness: "As the Father has sent Me, I also send you" (NASB).

## Forgiving and Retaining

We need go no further than the Day of Pentecost to see how the apostles forgave sins. On that day the Holy Spirit was sent by Christ and empowered the apostles in their preaching of the gospel. The Spirit brought conviction to the hearts of those who heard the message, and they cried out to Peter and the apostles, "What shall we do?" Peter then commanded them, "Repent, and let each of you be baptized in the name of Jesus Christ for the forgiveness of your sins; and you shall receive the gift of the Holy Spirit. . . . So then, those who had received his word were baptized; and there were added that day about three thousand souls" (Acts 2:37,38,41 NASB). Three thousand sinners were forgiven of their sins not by confessing their sins to the apostles, but by believing the gospel proclaimed by the apostles.

The gospel spread from Jerusalem to the Gentile world, where Peter continued to proclaim the good news of forgiveness of sins through Jesus Christ: "Through His name everyone who believes in Him receives forgiveness of sins" (Acts 10:43 NASB). Those who believed the good news that Jesus forgives sins put their faith in him and were "baptized in the name of Jesus Christ" (Acts 10:48 NASB).

The city of Antioch gave a very hostile reception to the gospel preached by the apostle Paul. The Jews who heard Paul were filled with jealousy and began contradicting him and uttering blasphemies. Paul turned to them and said, "Since you repudiate it, and judge yourselves unworthy of eternal life, behold, we are turning to the Gentiles." Taking his leave of them, Paul and his companions "shook off the dust of their feet in protest against them and went to Iconium" (Acts 13:46,51 NASB).

Paul's reception in the city of Athens was no more encouraging. There he was "solemnly testifying to the Jews that Jesus was the Christ." Scripture tells us that those who heard the message "resisted and blasphemed." To those who refused God's offer of forgiveness through his Christ, Paul "shook out his garments and said to them, 'Your blood be upon your own heads! I am clean. From now on I shall go to the Gentiles'" (Acts 18:5,6 NASB).

In both these cases the sins of those who rejected God's offer of forgiveness were retained, just as the sins of those who obeyed the gospel were forgiven. The response we make to the gospel determines whether our sins are forgiven or retained. The obedient are forgiven and the sins of the disobedient are retained.

**True Confession**

How are the sins we commit after our conversion forgiven? The Catholic Church says that one must go to confession and there confess all mortal sins to a priest in order to obtain absolution. In other words, the Church believes that the priest's role is indispensable to forgiveness. Searching for evidence to support that view in either the Scriptures or early church history is like looking for a nonexistent needle in a haystack. Only by staying with the teaching of the Scriptures can we know how sins are forgiven.

The apostle John speaks about the need to confess our sins, and his words have been a source of comfort to generations of God's people. Many a distraught soul has taken refuge in the truth he reveals. The confession that John speaks about bears no resemblance to the Catholic practice of telling one's sins to a priest. This is confession as revealed by the Holy Spirit to John:

> If we walk in the light as He Himself is in the light, we have fellowship with one another, and the blood of Jesus His Son cleanses us from all sin. . . . If we confess our sins, He is faithful and righteous to forgive us our sins and to cleanse us from all unrighteousness. . . . And if anyone sins, we have an Advocate with the Father, Jesus Christ the righteous (1 John 1:7–2:1 NASB).

Even after our conversion to Jesus we will be sinners; conversion is not designed to make us sinless on this earth. Every sin we will ever commit has been forgiven in the death of our Savior. In our daily walk with the Lord we confess our sins, not simply to notify God of something he would otherwise have been unaware of, but to acknowledge our dependence upon his grace and mercy. Though we are a forgiven people, we must also be a penitent people for having offended God. The need for one central human priest is dispensed with when we realize that *every* Christian is a priest and has direct access into the very presence of God through Jesus, our Great High Priest (1 Peter 2:5-9; Hebrews 10:19-22). Let us look at an apostolic example.

After Simon had been baptized, he sinned by trying to buy spiritual gifts. This was a serious matter, and Peter said to him, "Repent of this wickedness of yours, and pray the Lord that if possible, the intention of your heart may be forgiven you. For I see that you are in the gall of bitterness and in the bondage of iniquity" (Acts 8:22,23 NASB). Here we have a man who sinned after he had believed and been baptized. Yet Simon was not told to confess his sin to Peter or to anyone else to receive absolution. Peter mentioned nothing of the sort. Simon was told to *repent*—that is, to turn away from sin and pray to God for pardon.

Nothing in the ministry of the apostles even remotely resembles the Catholic sacrament of confession. It was only when the church drifted from its apostolic mooring, no longer holding to the Scriptures as its only source of authority, that religious innovations previously unknown took root and are with us to this day.

### Three Types of Confession

Is there ever an occasion when we must confess our sins to another person? If so, what are the circumstances? The Scriptures speak of confession in three categories: 1) secret confession between God and man alone, 2) private confession between two people, one of whom has been sinned against by the other party, and 3) public confession required in the exercise of church discipline.

When God alone is the offended party, then he alone is the one to whom confession should be made. The Scriptures speak of our "secret sins" (Psalm 90:8). These are the sins committed in the heart. Jesus speaks of this kind of secret sin: "I say to you that everyone who looks on a woman to lust for her has committed adultery with her already in his heart" (Matthew 5:28 NASB). These sins are to be confessed to God. No third party should be involved.

Not all sins are secret; some sins directly affect other people. In this case, private confession comes into play. It is not enough that we seek God's forgiveness; we must also seek the forgiveness of the person against whom we have sinned. This is one of the most neglected areas in the Christian life, though Jesus spoke clearly on the issue: "If therefore you are presenting your offering at the altar, and there remember that your brother has something against you, leave your offering there before the altar, and go your way; first be reconciled to your brother, and then come and present your offering" (Matthew 5:23,24 NASB). Jesus didn't tell the offender, "Go to confession." He told him to go and get matters straightened out with the one he had offended, to seek that person's forgiveness, and then to come back after having been forgiven and reconciled to that person.

As for someone who has sinned against us and comes seeking reconciliation, Jesus said, "If your brother sins, rebuke him; and if he repents, forgive him. And if he sins against you seven times a day, and returns to you seven times, saying, 'I repent,' forgive him" (Luke 17:3,4 NASB). Notice that the one who has been sinned against forgives the offender when the offender repents. The sign of repentance is that the offender goes to the brother he has offended and seeks his forgiveness. Forgiveness for all our sins must be sought from God. But when others are involved in our sins, we must seek their forgiveness also. We cannot be reconciled to God if we are not reconciled to our brother. This is confession ordained by Jesus and practiced by the early church.

The Lord's instructions on public confession in the Gospel of Matthew are very clear. If your brother sins against you, Jesus said, go and talk with him in private about the matter—just the two of you. If he repents, then you have won your brother. The matter is to go no further. But what if your brother will not repent? What is to happen then?

The next step is to bring one or two witnesses along with you. The matter has now moved from being private to being semiprivate. If this brother will not listen to them, then the third step is to be taken.

This final step involves the church—in this case the local congregation. If this brother refuses to listen to the church, who would appeal to him in a loving fashion to repent, then he is to be excluded from the fellowship of God's people (Matthew 18:15-17).

Of course, should he repent, the church must receive him back into fellowship. However, while he is impenitent his sins are retained. There is nothing in this whole discussion that even comes close to confession as practiced by Catholics. In fact, the words of Jesus forbid such a practice. Look closely at the procedure spoken of by Jesus. He said that if your brother sins against you, you yourself are to reprove him *in private*. If he repents, then the matter is to go no further. The only time someone else is to hear about the sin is when that brother refuses to repent. Then one or two witnesses are to be brought along.

The Catholic teaching says that even if two people are reconciled, the sin committed must also be confessed to a priest. That involves a third party, which is the very opposite of what Jesus said. Any teaching about confession of sins (especially the words of James, "Confess your sins to each other," [in James 5:16]) must be fulfilled within the boundaries set forth in Scripture.

## A Place for Guidance

Within the church there will always be Christians who need particular care and attention. At times these people may be the very backbone of the congregation, yet they may have occasional difficulty in coping with some sin in their life. While all sin must be confessed to God, that does not eliminate the supreme value of sharing our sins with someone who can help us. In fact, the Scriptures instruct us to watch out one for another. The mature have a responsibility to come to the rescue of those who struggle with their sins (Galatians 6:1,2). Needless burdens are sometimes carried by Christians who have not sought godly counsel from a mature Christian. Consider the following typical case.

John has been an active and faithful Christian for years. He is well-respected in the church and known for his good works. One of the leaders in the church can see that John is having some problems in his life. An appointment is made, and John tells of the turmoil that has been taking place in his life. He has been involved in an affair with another woman. He has spent sleepless nights worrying about his sin, even doubting if God could forgive him. He has sought God's pardon and knows that God has forgiven him, but his life is still shattered by what he did.

John will need the continual counseling of a godly Christian to help him get his life together again. In the process of receiving counseling, John may well reveal the details of the affair to his Christian counselor, but at no time is the counselor there as his confessor. He cannot give him absolution. He can, though, assure John that God has always promised to forgive the penitent and renew their lives again. John can receive invaluable instruction, guidance, and assurance from having spoken to a godly counselor about his sin. Such a practice has the endorsement of God.

## Our Forgiving God

The Lord is a forgiving God, anxious to pardon all who come to him. He is able to forgive us because of the death of his Son. The apostles were charged with proclaiming to all nations the good news of Jesus' death. Those who believed the claims of Jesus had their sins forgiven, while those who rejected the gospel had their sins retained.

At the moment of our conversion to Jesus we become a forgiven people, reconciled to God, adopted into his family. In Christ we enjoy the blessing of being continuously forgiven of all our sins. Not only are past sins forgiven, but the sins we will commit in the future have already been pardoned because of the death of God's Lamb. I want to stress this point to Roman Catholics: *Forgiveness of sins took place on the cross, not in confession.* Believers are part of the royal priesthood (1 Peter 2:9) and have direct access to the presence of God. At any time we can come to him in penitent prayer.

The strong stand taken by the Catholic Church on sin is commendable, especially in an age when sin is being explained out of existence by some theologians. However, the teaching of the Catholic Church on how our sins are forgiven is the point at which we must part company. The Scriptures we have discussed in this chapter reveal what the apostles and the early church taught about confession of sins. The forgiveness of our sins does not hinge on being given absolution by a priest. God alone knows our heart and absolves us of sin whenever and wherever we repent.

# CHAPTER 7

# Who Are God's Priests?

*T*he Catholic priest is indispensable to the sacramental life of the Roman Catholic Church. His ordination to the priesthood places an indelible mark upon his soul, thereby equipping him to celebrate Mass, hear confession, anoint the sick, etc.

This male priesthood is under attack from many quarters. Those within the priesthood have not been shy in highlighting its faults, and progressive-thinking women are vocal in demanding that they be included in what has been an exclusively male office. Attack and counterattack fly from those on both sides of the issue. Only a return to what the Bible has to say on this subject will provide the conclusive answer that many are seeking.

## The New Priesthood

The priesthood did not begin with the coming of the Christian faith. It has a long and distinguished pedigree spanning most of the Old Testament Scriptures. We first meet Israel's priests shortly after Israel left Egypt on their way to the Promised Land. From among the 12 tribes that composed the nation of Israel, God chose the tribe of Levi as the one from which the priests would come. Priesthood was therefore based strictly on ancestry. The function of a priest was to act on behalf of the people as their representative before God. This he did in his priestly role in the temple.

It was not God's intention that this type of priesthood should last forever. With the coming of Jesus, a priesthood would be established that would include all of God's people, not just a select few. Jesus brought in the new priesthood through his death upon the cross when he accomplished the forgiveness of our sins. His all-sufficient sacrifice eliminated forever the need for a priesthood to engage in offering any kind of sacrifice for our sins. The one sacrifice offered by Jesus our High Priest was accepted by the Father on our behalf (Hebrews 10:10-18).

The new priesthood which Jesus established is composed not of men born into the tribe of Levi, nor of Christian men only, but of all men and women who have been born anew (John 3:1-16). This is the "royal priesthood," the "kingdom of priests" referred to in the Scriptures by the apostles Peter and John (1 Peter 2:5; Revelation 1:6). We don't have to have a vocation or a special calling in order to be a priest. Neither must we undergo seven years of study in a seminary. Everyone who is a Christian is a priest, and the distinction between clergy and laity is without foundation.

That is why we never read in the New Testament of men being ordained as priests.

What we do find in Scripture are elders being appointed or ordained in local churches (Acts 14:23; Titus 1:5; 1 Timothy 3:1-7). Elders were appointed to care for the spiritual welfare of the local church (1 Peter 5:1-5). Their office is also referred to as pastor/bishop/overseer (Acts 20:17,28). It is incorrect to think that these elders were ordained as priests, as the Catholic Church sometimes maintains. Their appointment to this office was accompanied by the "laying on of hands" (1 Timothy 4:14; 5:22). This was the way the local church gave approval to the one being appointed. There was nothing "magical" or sacramental about this procedure.

The unique position of a Catholic priest cannot be maintained in the light of what the Scriptures teach. In the Old Testament there is abundant information pertaining to priests. They had to be from the right tribe, they wore special clothing designated by God, and the nature of their work was clearly set forth (Exodus 27–29; Leviticus 6:12; 10:11).

However, when we read about the life of the church in the New Testament, we don't find anything like the Roman Catholic priesthood. If such a priesthood were established by Christ, we should certainly expect to see some evidence of its existence, but none can be found in God's Word.

Unfortunately, the role of the Catholic priest resembles that of the priest in the Old Testament, who was robed in special vestments and offered sacrifices for the sins of the people. We have already seen that this type of priesthood was never intended to be permanent, but was replaced with a priesthood composed of all the men and women whom Jesus has saved. When a person becomes a Christian, he also becomes a priest who engages in offering spiritual sacrifices to God.

### The New Sacrifices

The priests in Christ's church offer a new kind of sacrifice. No longer is there a need for sacrifices to be offered for our sins. Instead, we are called upon "to offer your bodies as living sacrifices, holy and pleasing to God—this is your spiritual act of worship" (Romans 12:1). Let's look at some examples of spiritual sacrifices in the Bible.

The church in the city of Philippi was established by Paul on one of his missionary journeys. From the beginning a delightful relationship existed between them, and they were great supporters of Paul's evangelistic work. When Paul was imprisoned in Rome, they sent him gifts that would meet his needs. Courteous as always, Paul thanked them for their kindness, referring to their generosity as "a fragrant offering, an acceptable sacrifice, pleasing to God" (Philippians 4:18). Paul, in fact, thanked them for the priestly ministry they had rendered to him—a ministry which God accepted as a holy sacrifice.

On another occasion, Paul encouraged other Christians to continue engaging in their priestly duties of prayer and doing good because God views prayer offered by Christ's priests as sacrifice: "Through Jesus, therefore, let us continually offer to God a sacrifice of praise—the fruit of lips that confess his name" (Hebrews 13:15). The good works of service and charity which every Christian engages in are viewed as priestly sacrifices: "Do not forget to do good and to share with others," Paul says, "for with such sacrifices God is pleased" (Hebrews 13:16).

Emerging from the Scriptures is a lovely picture of what a Christian is: 1) a priest, 2) whose body is the temple of the Holy Spirit, and 3) who offers spiritual sacrifices to God (1 Peter 2:9; 1 Corinthians 6:19; Hebrews 13:15,16). Wherever there is a Christian, there is a priest and a temple in which spiritual sacrifices can be offered to God. This is the priesthood that Christ gave his church.

While every Christian is a priest, not every believer in the church has the same function as every other believer. For example, the leadership of the local church has been placed by God in the hands of men whom he has endowed with the necessary gifts to edify the body of Christ. Male leadership is a God-ordained structure for the church (1 Timothy 2:8-15). However, male leadership in no way reflects unfavorably upon Christian women, who are also heirs of salvation and have their own unique contributions to make to the life of the body of Christ.

## The Gift of Celibacy

Celibacy is a gift from God. Jesus taught that some have been given this gift for the benefit of the kingdom of heaven (Matthew 19:11,12).

Those who choose to be celibate for the sake of the kingdom of God have a distinct advantage, in some areas, over those who are married with families. I am thinking of just one example for which this advantage might apply. Suppose an opportunity arises for preaching the gospel in a remote and difficult area of the world and there are two suitable candidates for the job: One is celibate and the other is married with a young family. The obvious choice in this case is the one who will not be burdened with the responsibility of having to care for a family. The one who is celibate is free from having to worry about how his family will adjust to this new environment and whether there is suitable schooling for his children. The demands of such a pioneer work would be more suitable to someone who is celibate.

This is not to say that celibacy is a superior gift to marriage. It isn't. The work I am engaged in as an evangelist has been blessed by God through the support of my wife and three children. I would be greatly hampered if they were not in my life. In the early church the apostles were married—a fact that is never denied by the Catholic Church. However, we were taught that when the apostles said to the Lord, "We have left everything to follow you!" that included their wives (Matthew 19:27), and so celibacy made its entrance into the life of the church. I am amazed to think how naively so many of us accepted this as fact, never considering for a moment the grave injustice that such a decision would have imposed on the wives of the apostles.

Of course, such was never the case. Peter and the other apostles, along with the brothers of the Lord, remained married throughout their lives, and their wives often accompanied them on their journeys (1 Corinthians 9:3-5; cf. John 1:42). When Peter wrote about marriage he said, "Husbands, in the same way be considerate as you live with your wives, and treat them with respect" (1 Peter 3:7). Such instruction would sound very hollow indeed coming from a man who had himself left his wife. The text, Matthew 19:27, cited by the Catholic Church gives no credence to its teaching on celibacy.

The Catholic teaching on celibacy is in conflict with what is taught in Scripture. A man can be a priest whether he is married or celibate. Furthermore, a man holding the office of a bishop (who is also called an elder or pastor) is to be a married man. Paul explains that a bishop must be "the husband of but one wife. . . . He must manage his own family well and see that his children obey him with proper respect. If anyone does not know how to manage his own family, how can he take care of God's church?" (1 Timothy 3:1-5; cf. Titus 1:5-9).

The cover story for the February 23, 1970, issue of *Time* magazine was titled "The Catholic Exodus: Why Priests and Nuns are Quitting." Many of those who left their religious life expressed frustration with the lack of progress in the Catholic Church. Celibacy figured prominently in their dissatisfaction. Since those days, the number of priests who have left is in excess of 100,000. If you care to work it out, you will find, according to these figures, that a Catholic priest resigns his ministry every two hours. Something very serious must be wrong when the best-trained men in the Catholic Church are resigning in such large numbers.

## A Royal Priesthood

Many Catholics who have left the priesthood have found their spiritual life in the true church of Christ. I am personally acquainted with a number of men who have left the Catholic priesthood and have been truly converted to Jesus Christ. Their conversion to Christ their Savior has made them part of the royal priesthood of which Peter speaks (1 Peter 2:9).

These are not the first men to have left the priesthood. Luke records in the Bible how "the number of the disciples in Jerusalem increased rapidly, and a large number of priests became obedient to the faith" (Acts 6:7). These were Levitical priests who offered up daily sacrifices for the people. But on hearing the good news that the one sacrifice offered by Jesus achieved full forgiveness of all our sins, they became obedient to the Lord. They discontinued their former role as priests, seeing in Jesus Christ a superior priesthood and a superior sacrifice. Saved from their sins, they now became priests in the church of Christ, their former role having become redundant.

We will be nothing more or less than Christian priests when we return to the authority of the Scriptures for all that we believe and practice.

# CHAPTER 8

# *What About Mary?*

The history of Israel speaks of God making choices: Abraham was chosen to be the father of that nation, Judah was chosen to be the royal tribe, and the household of David was chosen to be the royal family. From the family of David, Mary was chosen to be the mother of Israel's Messiah—Jesus, the Son of God.

Many of these chosen people made a noble contribution to the work of God. They were people who remained faithful to God even under trying circumstances. The eleventh chapter of the Hebrew epistle holds up their faith as a model for us to imitate.

The faith of Mary is no exception. Her response to the news that she was to become the mother of the world's Savior was greeted not with protest, but with faithful submission: "May it be to me as you have said." In saying yes to God, Mary displayed a spirit that is worthy of imitation by every Christian. Unfortunately, the life of Mary as recorded in the Scriptures has been overshadowed by dogmas about her that are entirely man-made. They are teachings that actually distort the simplicity of Mary's story.

## Perpetual Virginity?

The perpetual virginity of Mary is a major Marian doctrine. While the Scriptures clearly teach the virgin birth of Jesus, they never support the notion that Mary was always a virgin. The perpetual virginity of Mary is a man-made doctrine. An examination of Scripture compels us to believe that Mary did not remain a virgin after she gave birth to Jesus. But first let us hear what the Catholic Church teaches on this subject.

> Q. 5 Did Christ have brothers and sisters?
>
> No. The marriage between Joseph and Mary was always completely virginal. Following Jewish usage, the brethren of Christ mentioned in the gospels were merely his cousins or other distant relatives.
>
> Q. 6 How do we know that Mary remained always a virgin?
>
> We are certain of it because God, speaking to us through the inspired Scriptures and through His infallible Church, tells us it is true.[1]

These are clear, unambiguous statements, leaving no room for anyone to misunderstand exactly where the Catholic Church stands on this issue. But is it in harmony with the teaching of the Bible?

## The Testimony of Matthew

Joseph and Mary were engaged to be married. When Joseph found that Mary was pregnant, he planned to divorce her quietly. His plans were interrupted by an angel, who told him that the child that Mary was carrying was from the Holy Spirit. Matthew says, "When Joseph woke up, he did what the angel of the Lord had commanded him and took Mary home as his wife. But he had no union with her until she gave birth to a son. And he gave him the name Jesus" (Matthew 1:24,25).

Matthew is careful to point out that Joseph could not have been the father of Jesus. The wording used by Matthew insists that while Joseph and Mary lived together as husband and wife during her pregnancy, they had no sexual relations until after Jesus was born. Matthew needs to stress that point because later he speaks of the brothers and sisters of Jesus born to Mary and Joseph (Matthew 12:46,47; 13:53-57).

I need to make a point here. There is nothing unholy about Mary and Joseph having intercourse. How could there be? Marriage was designed by God, with sex as one of its blessings. It must be remembered that Joseph and Mary were engaged to be married. Like any engaged couple, they may have discussed, among other matters, the subject of sex. Such a discussion would not have been unholy.

The place of sex within the bounds of marriage has the endorsement of God. The notion of marriage without sex is the opposite of what the Scriptures teach: "Marriage should be honored by all, and the marriage bed kept pure, for God will judge the adulterer and all the sexually immoral" (Hebrews 13:4).

The apostle Paul is very outspoken about the place of sex in marriage and the mutual obligation of both husband and wife to fulfill the sexual desires of their partner. "The husband should fulfill his marital duty to his wife," Paul says, "and likewise the wife to her husband. The wife's body does not belong to her alone but also to her husband. In the same way, the husband's body does not belong to him alone but also to his wife. Do not deprive each other except by mutual consent and for a time, so that you may devote yourselves to prayer. Then come together again so that Satan will not tempt you because of your lack of self-control" (1 Corinthians 7:3-5).

Within the bounds of their marriage Joseph and Mary had sex. This harmonized with the will of God. Not to have sex within marriage is to reject what God approves. Mark, the writer of the Gospel that bears his name, does not endorse the Roman Catholic teaching. He believed that Mary did not remain a virgin all her life.

## The Testimony of Mark

The ministry of Jesus caused ripples on the waters. In fact, quite a storm gathered, and he found himself in frequent conflict with the religious authorities. His family were none too pleased with the publicity he was receiving, so something had to be done. When he arrived at a house where a crowd had gathered to meet him, his family heard about this and "they went to take charge of him, for they said, 'He is out of his mind'" (Mark 3:21).

When he finished teaching, "Jesus' mother and brothers arrived. Standing outside, they sent someone in to call him. A crowd was sitting around him, and told him, 'Your mother and brothers are outside looking for you.' 'Who are my mother and brothers?' he asked. Then he looked at those seated in a circle around him and said, 'Here are my mother and brothers! Whoever does God's will is my brother and sister and mother'" (Mark 3:31-34). If the perpetual virginity of Mary were true, Jesus had the perfect opportunity to set the record straight by telling those around him that he didn't have any brothers or sisters— that he was an only child. But he didn't!

Mark provides additional information about the brothers and sisters of Jesus. The reaction that Jesus received to his teachings and miracles was one of amazement and unbelief. "Where did this man get these things?" they asked. "What's this wisdom that has been given him, that he even does miracles! Isn't this the carpenter? Isn't this Mary's son and the brother of James, Joseph, Judas and Simon? Aren't his sisters here with us?" (Mark 6:1-3). Certainly the people of Nazareth believed that Jesus had brothers and sisters, and they were in the best position to know. So why not accept their testimony?

Their astonishment about Jesus arose from the fact that he was so ordinary. He was a local tradesman with brothers and sisters like everyone else. Yet he was claiming to be the fulfillment of all that the prophets had written about. No wonder "they took offense at him" (Mark 6:3).

## The Testimony of Luke

Luke, the beloved physician, also has something important to say on the subject. The opening paragraph of Luke's Gospel tells how thoroughly he researched his work before writing his Gospel (Luke 1:1-4). Many eyewitnesses, who could be interviewed and who could verify the facts, were still alive. Mary was the most obvious source for Luke's information about circumstances surrounding the birth of Jesus Christ. Based on his careful research, Luke set forth the virgin birth as a fact (Luke 1:26-38). The evidence must have been compelling for a doctor to believe it.

At the same time, Luke had no reservations in stating that Mary did have other children (Luke 8:19-21). When Luke wrote the Acts of the Apostles, he once again affirmed that Mary had other children apart from Jesus. He tells us that the apostles had gathered in the upper room awaiting the Day of Pentecost. "They all joined together constantly in prayer, along with the women and Mary the mother of Jesus, and with his brothers" (Acts 1:14). Luke, who was a careful historian and a physician, believed in the virgin birth of Christ, but denied that Mary was a virgin all of her life. His testimony cannot be dismissed lightly.

## The Testimony of John

The testimony of John is important since he spent considerable time with the Lord and would have been in the company of Mary on many occasions. His close association with Jesus gave him firsthand knowledge of the family of the Lord. In the Gospel that bears his name and in his epistles John vigorously defends the Lord's deity. He sets forth the incarnation as a fact and affirms that Jesus is God the Son, the second Person of the Blessed Trinity (John 1:1-18; 10:30-36; 14:15-31).

John believed that Jesus was born of a virgin named Mary, but he never believed that Mary remained a virgin throughout her life. After Jesus had changed the water into wine, John records that Jesus "went down to Capernaum with his mother and brothers and his disciples" (John 2:12).

Three times in one short paragraph John mentions the Lord's brothers: "When the Jewish Feast of Tabernacles was near, Jesus' brothers said to him...For even his own brothers did not believe in him....However, after his brothers had left for the Feast, he went also, not publicly, but in secret" (John 7:2,3,5,10). Statements like this could not have been made unless Mary was the mother of several children.

### The Testimony of Paul

The great apostle Paul (who wrote over half of the New Testament Scriptures) never believed in the perpetual virginity of Mary. Quite the contrary, for Paul recalls meeting James, the brother of Jesus. "Then after three years," Paul says, "I went up to Jerusalem to get acquainted with Peter and stayed with him fifteen days. I saw none of the other apostles—only James, the Lord's brother." Immediately following that statement Paul says, "I assure you before God that what I am writing you is no lie" (Galatians 1:18-20).

In defending his right to be financially supported by the church for his work, Paul says, "This is my defense to those who sit in judgment on me. Don't we have the right to food and drink? Don't we have the right to take a believing wife along with us, as do the other apostles and the Lord's brothers and Cephas?" (1 Corinthians 9:3-5). Based on the evidence from Scripture, we simply cannot believe that Mary was always a virgin.

### The Catholic Reply

Someone might ask, "If the evidence is so compelling, why does the Catholic Church not believe it? Why are they so blind if it is as plain as it appears?" We must remember that the Catholic Church is not dependent upon the Scriptures alone for their teachings; they also draw from another source—the tradition of their Church. The doctrine of the perpetual virginity of Mary is one of those teachings that is based not on Scripture but on the sources that take us outside of what the Scriptures say.

The Catholic Church defends the doctrine of the perpetual virginity by saying that the church has always believed it to be true (which is incorrect) and that any reference to the Lord's brothers and sisters is a reference to his cousins.

## The Biblical Answer

There is in fact only one word used in the Greek New Testament for describing brothers and sisters, relatives, or fellow Jews. So how are we to know the meaning of this word when we read it in the Bible? *By the context in which it is found.*

Speaking to the thousands of Jews who had come to Jerusalem for the Feast of Pentecost, Peter referred to them as "brothers" (Acts 2:29). Paul, in defending himself against hostile Jews, referred to them in similar fashion: "brothers" (Acts 22:1). The context in both of these cases determines how the word "brothers" is to be understood: as a reference to their common ancestry, their common descent from the same father, Abraham.

When the angel Gabriel announced to Mary that she was to be the mother of the Messiah, the angel also told her that her cousin Elizabeth, who was advanced in years, was now six months pregnant (Luke 1:36,58). How do we know that Elizabeth was not Mary's actual sister, but her cousin? The context in which the discussion takes place leaves no doubt that Elizabeth was not just a fellow Jew but was in fact also her cousin.

When reference is made to the brothers and sisters of Jesus, how do we know that it is not a reference to their common ancestry, or a reference to his cousins or relatives? As we look at the context in which the statement is made, we find compelling evidence that Jesus did in fact have brothers and sisters. Certainly this is what was believed by Matthew, Mark, Luke, John, and Paul. They did not believe in the perpetual virginity of Mary.

Some readers might think that this whole discussion is nothing more than an irrelevant debate. But it is not, because at the heart of the discussion lies our fundamental attitude toward religious authority: Do we accept the Bible as our only authority, or do we accept the Catholic position of taking both Scripture and tradition? The Catholic Church cannot defend its doctrine from the Bible; it must go outside the Word of God, and as a result it ends up with a doctrine that contradicts what the Word of God clearly teaches.

If the doctrine of the perpetual virginity of Mary had originated with God, we would find corroborating evidence in the Scriptures. But no such evidence exists, and the testimony of Scripture compels us to believe that Mary had other children from her marriage with Joseph.

## Immaculate Conception?

On December 8, 1854, Pope Pius IX issued the following decree:

> We, by the authority of Jesus Christ, our Lord, of the Blessed Apostles, Peter and Paul and by our Own, declare, pronounce, and define that the doctrine which holds that the Blessed Virgin Mary, at the first instant of her conception, by a singular privilege and grace of the omnipotent God, in consideration of the merits of Jesus Christ, the Savior of mankind was preserved free from all stain of original sin, has been revealed by God, and therefore is to be firmly and constantly believed by all the faithful.[2]

This Papal decree collides with several Popes who repudiated the doctrine.

Aniceto Sparagna, a former Roman Catholic priest, has documented the opposition of many church fathers and some early Popes to this doctrine. Included are St. Bernard, St. Augustine, St. Peter Lombard, St. Albert the Great, St. Thomas Aquinas, and St. Antonius. He also documents statements by several Popes which either directly or indirectly show that they never believed in the Immaculate Conception. For example:

Pope Leo I (440): "The Lord Jesus Christ alonè among the sons of men was born immaculate" (Sermon 24 in *Nativ. Dom.*).

Pope Gelasius (492): "It belongs alone to the Immaculate Lamb to have no sin at all" (*Gelassii Papae Dicta*, vol. 4, col. 1241, Paris, 1671).

Pope Innocent III (1216): "She [Eve] was produced without sin, but she brought forth in sin; she [Mary] was produced in sin, but she brought forth without sin" (*De Festo Assump.*, sermon 2).[3]

## The Catholic Reply

What evidence from Scripture can the Catholic Church produce to support the Immaculate Conception? In the Papal decree of 1854 two Scriptures were cited. Genesis 3:15 says, "I will put enmity between you and the woman, and between your offspring and hers; he will crush your head, and you will strike his heel." This is not a reference to Mary, though pictures and statues portray her as crushing the head of the serpent. Genesis 3:15 is a prophecy about Jesus, who descended from a woman, and who would defeat Satan. The Scriptures support this view: "The reason the Son of God appeared was to destroy the devil's work" (1 John 3:8). Furthermore, "by his death he might destroy him who had the power of death—that is, the devil" (Hebrews 2:14). Catholic teaching can find no support for its doctrine in this section of God's Word.

The second Scripture in the Papal decree is Luke 1:28, which speaks of Mary as being "full of grace" or "highly favored." This expression has no reference whatsoever to Mary's supposed sinlessness. She was chosen by a gracious act of God to be the mother of the Lord. In that respect she is indeed "highly favored." Because of her unique privilege every generation will call her blessed. (Blessed is not a religious title; it speaks of the privilege given to Mary in being chosen to give birth to Jesus).

The expression "full of grace" appears only twice in the New Testament Scriptures. The second occurrence is in Ephesians 1:5-8, where Paul speaks of all Christians as being full of grace. Paul is teaching that all Christians are the recipients of God's grace. Our relationship with God results from God being gracious to us. His grace is an unmerited and undeserved favor that he bestows upon us. Therefore we are all "full of grace." Nothing more nor less is implied in these words.

The Immaculate Conception as set forth by Pope Pius IX was an unknown doctrine to his predecessors. And so is the doctrine that teaches Mary's sinlessness.

## What the Scriptures Say

If Mary's sinlessness is a revelation from God, we would expect Scripture to affirm it, or at least not to contain any statements that would be in conflict with this new revelation. Before examining the testimony of the Scriptures, some groundwork needs to be laid.

First, when God wanted to say that an exception to the rule existed, he made this perfectly plain. For example, Jesus taught that marriage was a lifelong bond. He didn't leave it at that, however, but stated the one exception to that rule: adultery. "I tell you," he said, "that anyone who divorces his wife, *except* for marital unfaithfulness, and marries another woman commits adultery" (Matthew 19:9).

Second, Christians believe that we are all sinners; no serious dispute exists on this point. Jesus himself is the only exception to that rule; he was without sin. Scripture tells us that Jesus was "tempted in every way, just as we are—*yet was without sin*" (Hebrews 4:15). From these two examples we can see that when there is an exception to a rule, God states it.

Both the apostles Paul and John exclude any possibility of an Immaculate Conception. Guided by the Holy Spirit of truth, they declare:

> There is no one righteous, not even one (Romans 3:10).

All have sinned and fall short of the glory of God (Romans 3:23).

If we claim to be without sin, we deceive ourselves and the truth is not in us (1 John 1:8).

If we claim we have not sinned, we make him [God] out to be a liar, and his word has no place in our lives (1 John 1:10).

## The Testimony of Mary

The testimony of Mary harmonizes with the whole tenor of Scripture. If we could ask her, "Do you believe in the doctrine of the Immaculate Conception?" she would disclaim belief in that doctrine in the following way.

First, when Mary visited her cousin Elizabeth and was greeted as the mother of the Lord, Mary responded by saying, "My soul glorifies the Lord and my spirit rejoices in God my Savior" (Luke 1:46,47). On the testimony of Mary's own words, she acknowledges her need for a Savior. Who needs a Savior? *Sinners* do. Mary was in the best position to know whether she was a sinner or not.

Second, Mary's actions after Jesus' birth show that she believed herself to be a sinner. After the birth of Jesus the time of her purification arrived, and she went to the temple and offered the appropriate sacrifices that were commanded in the law of Moses. The offering of the sacrifices made Mary ceremonially clean. They also identified her as a sinner, a fact which she did not deny.

The law of Moses contained the following instruction: "These are the regulations for the woman who gives birth to a boy or a girl. If she cannot afford a lamb, she is to bring two doves or two young pigeons, one for a burnt offering and the other for a sin offering" (Leviticus 12:7,8; cf. Luke 2:22-24). Mary complied with the law of Moses and offered her sin offering because she knew that she was a sinner in need of a Savior. We pay her no honor by saying otherwise, no matter how good our intentions may be.

## The Assumption of Mary

On November 1, 1950, Pope Pius XII made an *ex cathedra* pronouncement declaring the Assumption to be an infallible doctrine of the Catholic Church:

> By the authority of our Lord Jesus Christ, of the Blessed Apostles Peter and Paul, and by our own authority, we pronounce, declare, and define it to be a dogma divinely revealed: that the Immaculate Mother of God, Mary ever virgin, on the completion of her earthly life, was assumed to heavenly glory both in body and soul. Wherefore if anyone presume (which God forbid) wilfully to deny or call into doubt what has been defined by us, let him know that he has fallen away entirely from the divine and Catholic faith.[4]

That is a strong statement! This doctrine is said to be of divine origin, with severe consequences for those who reject it. We would expect a generous supply of evidence to be forthcoming for this doctrine, but, as with the Immaculate Conception, the Assumption also lacks any basis in the Scriptures.

## The Biblical Response

Before Jesus ascended to heaven, he promised to send the Holy Spirit to the apostles. The Spirit would guide them, teach them, and recall to their minds all that Jesus had taught them during his life (John 14:26; 16:13). They in turn wrote down what they had been taught as they were guided by the Spirit of truth. What they wrote in Scripture was sufficient. "His divine power," Peter says, "has given us everything we need for life and godliness" (2 Peter 1:3).

Paul assured the Christian believers that he had made known to them everything that God had to say. Yet he never mentioned the Assumption. "You know," Paul says, "that I have not hesitated to preach anything that would be helpful to you. . . . For I have not hesitated to proclaim to you the whole will of God" (Acts 20:20,27). In reading the Scriptures, we find no mention of the Assumption. Obviously it was not part of anything that Jesus ever taught, nor was it a doctrine ever believed by the apostles.

The apostle John, who was entrusted with the care of Mary by the Lord himself, wrote five books in the New Testament. Not once does he even hint at the doctrine of the Assumption. The silence of the Scriptures cannot be ignored on this matter; every doctrine of the early church is firmly rooted in the Scriptures. For example, the virgin birth of Christ was foretold by the prophets and its fulfillment is recorded in the Scriptures. Yet neither the Immaculate Conception nor the Assumption are foretold or recorded as having occurred. If these doctrines were important (or even true at all), they would have been recorded in the Scriptures.

On the Day of Pentecost, Peter proclaimed the good news that Jesus had risen in victory from the grave and had ascended to the Father's right hand in heaven: "Seeing what was ahead, he [the prophet David] spoke of the resurrection of the Christ, that he was not abandoned to the grave, nor did his body see decay. God has raised this Jesus to life, and we are all witnesses of the fact" (Acts 2:31,32; cf. Psalm 16:9,10).

Unlike Christ's body, our bodies all undergo decay when we die. Our resurrection is a future event, and the victory of the risen Christ guarantees this resurrection. Paul says that Jesus is the "firstfruits" from the dead. The "first fruits" is an agricultural expression which speaks of a coming harvest. "For as in Adam all die, so in Christ all will be made alive. But each in his own turn: Christ, the firstfruits; then, when he comes, those who belong to him" (1 Corinthians 15:22,23). This is plain language. The resurrection of the dead, without exception, will not occur until the Lord returns.

Therefore the Papal claim that the Assumption of Mary is "a dogma divinely revealed" must be rejected because it is in conflict with the truth that God has divinely revealed in Scripture.

## Intercession by Mary?

Father John Walsh, S.J., having set forth the Catholic doctrine of the Assumption, sees the intercession of Mary as the next logical step. He both asks and answers the following question:

> Q. Now that she is in heaven, does the Blessed Mother pay any attention to men on earth?
>
> A. Since her son died for all men, Mary is keenly interested in the welfare of every man and woman on earth. She regards us all as her children and continually prays for us.[5]

For many years I had a fervent devotion to Mary and believed all that the Catholic Church taught about her. I said prayers to Our Lady, did many novenas in her honor, and said the Rosary daily. The intercession of Mary was a vital part of my religious experience. Testimonies to the effectiveness of her intercession abounded.

The practice was reinforced with simple illustrations from everyday life. For instance, when you want to borrow the car for the evening, what do you do? You ask your mother to have a word with your father, and in no time at all you are driving off to an evening's entertainment. The application of this illustration was irresistible. If a mother can secure our request on earth, will not Mary, who is our mother in heaven, secure spiritual help for all her children? The notion that her Son would refuse a request from his own mother was unthinkable. We never questioned the validity of this reasoning. It all seemed so logical.

## True Biblical Intercession

However, this Marian doctrine runs into difficulty in two areas. First, the doctrine of the Assumption of Mary's body and soul into heaven has been shown to be without foundation. Second, Scripture instructs us to address our prayers only to God.

The scales fell from my eyes when I saw the sufficiency of the Lord Jesus Christ to meet my needs. Like many sincere Roman Catholics, my concept of God was inadequate. I honestly felt that my prayers had a better chance of being answered if I prayed to Mary. Of course, I also had a long list of saints whom I called upon from time to time to meet the crisis of the hour. The epistle to the Hebrews was the door that opened the wonder of the Lord to me.

This epistle presents Jesus as being able to identify with all of our needs. His life on earth exposed him to every conceivable struggle and temptation that we have to face. He experienced rejection and the deep hurt of betrayal. He was not immune to the cruel slander that religious leaders spread about him. On more than one occasion his feelings were hurt by the ingratitude of people he had helped. He knew what it was like to have to struggle against the temptations of Satan.

In what way do his struggles help us today? It was Scriptures like the following that moved my soul to rejoice in the sufficiency of the Lord:

> Because he himself suffered when he was tempted, he is able to help those who are being tempted (Hebrews 2:18).

> We do not have a high priest who is unable to sympathize with our weaknesses, but we have one who has been tempted in every way, just as we are—yet without sin. Let us then approach the throne of grace with confidence, so that we may receive mercy and find grace to help us in our time of need (Hebrews 4:15,16).

> He is able to save completely those who come to God through him, because he always lives to intercede for them (Hebrews 7:25).

What do these Scriptures tell us about the Lord? They tell us that Jesus is adequate to meet all our needs. When we pray we do not petition a reluctant God, but a loving Father whose Son has identified himself with our trials and tribulations. As our High Priest, Jesus is sympathetic to each of us and intercedes for us through his priestly ministry. Because Jesus has complete power, full understanding, and the willingness to come to our aid, there is no need for the intercession of Mary or the saints.

## Christ's Invitation

Jesus extends an invitation to all people who struggle and are in need: "Come to me, all you who are weary and burdened, and I will give you rest. Take my yoke upon you and learn from me, for I am gentle and humble in heart, and you will find rest for your souls. For my yoke is easy and my burden is light" (Matthew 11:28-30). There is no need that he will not meet, no problem he will not solve, no crisis too big for him to handle, and no person too sinful for him to help. He issues his invitation to the hurting people of this world. He bids them come to *him*, not to Mary.

When Jesus was asked by his disciples to teach them to pray, he taught them the Lord's Prayer, not the Rosary (Luke 11:1-4). In this prayer, God is the One to whom all prayer is directed and the One who is able to meet all of our needs. Jesus never told people to pray to Mary or to any of the worthy men and women of the past, such as Abraham, Moses, or David. Prayer is a sacrifice we offer to *God*. It is an act of worship, and God alone is to be worshiped (Hebrews 13:15,16; Matthew 4:10). To pray to anyone other than God is to engage in false worship, and that is idolatry, which is a violation of God's will.

## The Queen of Heaven

In justifying the practice of praying to Mary (or to the saints, for that matter), the argument is presented this way: Many people testify that when they have prayed to Mary their requests have been answered, and therefore the practice must be legitimate. However, consider the practice of the nation of Israel when they prayed to the Queen of Heaven in the days of the prophet Jeremiah. The people justified their practice on the grounds that when they stopped praying to the Queen of Heaven, everything went wrong for them. Conversely, when they prayed to her, everything in their lives went right:

> We will burn incense to the Queen of Heaven and will pour out drink offerings to her just as we and our fathers, our kings and our officials did in the towns of Judah and in the streets of Jerusalem. At that time we had plenty of food and were well off and suffered no harm. But ever since we stopped burning incense to the Queen of Heaven and pouring out drink offerings to her, we have had nothing and have been perishing by sword and famine (Jeremiah 44:17,18).

This was a practice which offended God and against which Jeremiah spoke out courageously. But his words fell on deaf ears. The people preferred to follow their own judgment rather than God's.

### The Wedding in Cana

The Catholic Church is quick to point to the wedding feast in Cana in order to justify the practice of praying to Mary (John 2:1-11). But a fair examination of the event and its context will not support that Catholic claim. At the wedding in Cana, Mary told Jesus that they had run out of wine. Did this information startle him? Had she told him something he didn't know? Certainly not! He is God the Son and knows all things. Then why did she tell him? She knew who Jesus was and that he was able to meet the need of the hour. Therefore Mary told the servants to carry out whatever Jesus instructed. They did, and he turned the water into wine.

There is absolutely nothing in this story that would give any fair-minded person the impression that it is legitimate to pray to Mary today on the basis of this event. To reach that conclusion we must take the whole story out of its context and give it a meaning other than that intended by John when he recorded the incident.

## Promises from God

There is nothing Mary can do for us that Jesus has not promised to do. Why would we need the intercession of Mary when we have the following promises from the Lord?

> Ask and it will be given to you; seek and you will find; knock and the door will be opened to you. For everyone who asks receives; he who seeks finds; and to him who knocks, the door will be opened. Which of you, if his son asks for bread, will give him a stone? Or if he asks for a fish, will give him a snake? If you, then, though you are evil, know how to give good gifts to your children, how much more will your Father in heaven give good gifts to those who ask him! (Matthew 7:7-11).

> I will do whatever you ask in my name, so that the Son may bring glory to the Father. You may ask me for anything in my name, and I will do it (John 14:13,14).

> Dear friends, if our hearts do not condemn us, we have confidence before God and receive from him anything we ask, because we obey his commands and do what pleases him (1 John 3:21,22).

> This is the confidence we have in approaching God: that if we ask anything according to his will, he hears us. And if we know that he hears us— whatever we ask—we know that we have what we asked of him (1 John 5:14,15).

> My God will meet all your needs according to his glorious riches in Christ Jesus (Philippians 4:19).

> The Spirit helps us in our weakness. We do not know what we ought to pray for, but the Spirit himself intercedes for us with groans that words cannot express. And he who searches our hearts

knows the mind of the Spirit, because the Spirit intercedes for the saints in accordance with God's will (Romans 8:26,27).

## Apparitions of Mary

Devotion to the Blessed Virgin Mary has been accelerated by her alleged apparitions in Fatima, Lourdes, and Guadalupe. Her message is one of peace for the world, and a call for more people to say the Rosary. These and other places have become places of pilgrimage for millions of Catholics, especially those who are sick, terminally ill, or physically handicapped; they come from all around the world hoping to be cured. At these places of pilgrimage, many cures and a number of miracles have been reported.

What is the biblical response to such apparitions, visions, miracles, healings, and cures? Are they true, or is the whole thing a hoax?

The only safe ground upon which we can place our feet is the Word of God. We must compare the claims of Lourdes and elsewhere with what we find in the Bible and then weigh the evidence.

Strategically placed throughout the entire Bible are warnings from God about the appearing of false miracles, signs, and wonders. Spectacular though they are, they do not originate with God. Some of these wonders will closely resemble what God does, but are detected as false because of the message that accompanies them. Because a great wonder has happened is not sufficient reason to believe that it came from God, even if we cannot give a definitive explanation as to how it happened. Truth is measured not by apparitions alone, but by the message that accompanies the alleged apparition.

Let us look at some of the warnings God has given to keep us from straying from his truth revealed in Scripture.

## False Visions and Miracles

Many false religions have appealed to their alleged miracles and to the visions received by their founders in order to support their particular teachings—teachings that directly contradict what God has already revealed. God gave the nation of Israel strict warning to avoid those people whose message is contrary to what he said, even when the message of the false teacher was accompanied by some great sign and wonder.

> If a prophet, or one who foretells by dreams, appears among you and announces to you a miraculous sign or wonder, and if the sign or wonder of which he has spoken takes place, and he says, "Let us follow other gods" (gods you have not known) "and let us worship them," you must not listen to the words of that prophet or dreamer. The Lord your God is testing you to find out whether you love him with all your heart and with all your soul. It is the Lord your God you must follow, and him you must revere. Keep his commands and obey him; serve him and hold fast to him (Deuteronomy 13:1-4).

God is telling his people that a distinct possibility exists of a miracle, sign, or wonder being performed, but that the message from the one who does such wonders is contrary to the will of God. The message of Lourdes is one that contradicts the Word of God. The Bible teaches us to have devotion only to the Lord, and to pray only to him, yet the message of Lourdes violates this. Listen to the warning Jesus gives:

> False Christs and false prophets will appear and perform great signs and miracles to deceive even the elect—if that were possible (Matthew 24:24).

We have clear warnings from Jesus, who saw the distinct possibility of miracles coming from people whose teachings are in fact false. We will know if a message is from God when it harmonizes with what God has already revealed. Lourdes distracts from Christ and turns people's hearts to having greater devotion to Mary.

Here are two warnings given to the church by the apostle Paul:

> I am afraid that just as Eve was deceived by the serpent's cunning, your minds may somehow be led astray from your sincere and pure devotion to Christ (2 Corinthians 11:3).

> Satan himself masquerades as an angel of light (2 Corinthians 11:14).

One particular passage of God's Word always reminds me of the danger of false miracles:

> The coming of the lawless one will be in accordance with the work of Satan displayed in all kinds of counterfeit miracles, signs and wonders, and in every sort of evil that deceives those who are perishing. They perish because they refused to love the truth and so be saved. For this reason God sends them a powerful delusion so that they will believe the lie and so that all will be condemned who have not believed the truth but have delighted in wickedness (2 Thessalonians 2:9-12).

The apostle John in the book of Revelation depicts the church as victorious, yet facing great persecution. One of the enemies of the church is the false doctrines that come from the devil and his fallen angels. It is significant that *these doctrines are accompanied by miracles.* Because miracles are being performed, should we then believe the doctrines to be true? Of course not!

> He [the second beast] performed great and miraculous signs, even causing fire to come down from heaven to earth in full view of men (Revelation 13:13).

The activities of Simon the sorcerer teach us that even bright, intelligent people can be fooled into thinking that something is from God when in fact it is not. Listen to what the Word of God has to say:

> For some time a man named Simon had practiced sorcery in the city and amazed all the people of Samaria. He boasted that he was someone great, and all the people, both high and low, gave him their attention and exclaimed, "This man is the divine power known as the Great Power." They followed him because he had amazed them for a long time with his magic (Acts 8:9-11).

## Paul's Warning

Paul's warning in Galatians is worthy of our close attention. Paul does not dismiss the possibility of a person having a vision. If someone had told Paul that he or she had seen a vision, I don't think he would have argued that point. However, if that person went on to say that the vision said we were to say the Rosary and have greater devotion to Mary, then Paul would have had no hesitation in condemning the message as totally false. That is what he did when defending the gospel against the infiltration of falsehood:

> Even if we or an angel from heaven should preach a gospel other than the one we preached to you, let him be eternally condemned! As we have already said, so now I say again: If anybody is preaching to you a gospel other than what you accepted, let him be eternally condemned! (Galatians 1:8,9).

Let me state this as simply as possible: *Miracles in and of themselves prove nothing.* The devil can work miracles, and his demonic forces are involved in the working of signs and wonders in the world today. So where does that leave us? We must arrive at truth not by believing only in miracles, but by measuring the message against what God himself has said. Only then will we know whether something is true or false.

# CHAPTER 9

# *What About Purgatory?*

*T*he family, a father and his young children, occupied the front seat in the church. On the center aisle lay the coffin containing the remains of a beloved wife and caring mother. She had been a good and kindly lady, respected by all who knew her. Death, that uninvited intruder, had taken her life and shattered the fragile world of her family. Their gentle sobbing echoed around the large church.

The ringing of altar bells announced that the priest was ready to say Mass on behalf of the deceased. He spent a few moments with the family, then announced to the congregation that this Mass was being offered for the repose of the soul of their departed loved one who was now in purgatory. Through the holy sacrifice of the Mass, her soul would eventually be released from the pain of purgatory.

Purgatory is a doctrine woven into the teachings of the Catholic Church. Belief in purgatory is strong, as evidenced by the many Masses that family and friends have offered for those who have died. Have you ever wondered why there should be a need for purgatory, and if there is any evidence for its existence?

## Paid in Full by Christ

Purgatory does nothing to honor the achievements of Christ's death. It says, in effect, that his death did not achieve a full pardon for our sins and that his suffering and death must be supplemented by our own suffering in purgatory. This doctrine contradicts the plain teachings of Scripture and does not acknowledge the redemptive power of the cross of Christ. I share the view of the great apostle Paul, who said that Jesus "is able to save completely those who come to God through him, because he always lives to intercede for them" (Hebrews 7:25). Since Jesus completely saves us, there is no need for purgatory.

When we understand fully that the sacrifice of Christ achieved the pardon of all our sins, purgatory becomes a redundant doctrine. Knowing that Jesus paid our debt should stir in us a spirit of worship and adoration of Christ the Lord. Let us start at the beginning.

Joseph was told that Mary's child was to be named Jesus "because he will save his people from their sins" (Matthew 1:21). What does it mean to be saved from our sins? It means that the death of Jesus paid the penalty incurred by our sins, freeing us from the condemnation and punishment that our sins deserve. God now treats us as if we had never sinned. That's the gospel! That's the good news that God has announced from heaven!

The consequence of our sins can be seen in our Lord's use of the word "ransom." Jesus said he did not come to be served, "but to serve, and give his life as a ransom for many" (Matthew 20:28). The word "ransom" brings to mind hostages, whose release is secured when payment has been made. Similarly, our freedom from the penalty of our sins was secured upon the payment of the death of God the Son. Peter reinforces this point when he says that we have been redeemed "with the precious blood of Christ, a lamb without blemish or defect" (1 Peter 1:19). John echoes the same truth when he says that Jesus "freed us from our sins by his blood" (Revelation 1:5). In his epistle, he says that "the blood of Jesus, his Son, purifies us from all sin"

(1 John 1:7). The sins that once awaited punishment have now been pardoned. God now treats us, his children, as if we had never sinned.

Peter wrote one of my favorite verses of Scripture. He says, "For Christ died for sins once for all, the righteous for the unrighteous, to bring you to God" (1 Peter 3:18). I love that expression "to bring you to God." The death of Jesus accomplished what it was intended to do: bring us back to God.

"Mission Accomplished" can be written over the cross of Christ. Divine justice has been fully satisfied. The Lamb of God has opened the way back to the Father. That is why Jesus said, "I am the way and the truth and the life. No one comes to the Father except through me" (John 14:6). Jesus is the Good Shepherd who saves his sheep by laying down his life for them. "I have come," he says, "that they may have life, and have it to the full" (John 10:10). Jesus is the giver of life to the spiritually dead. He is the One who forgives our sins. He is the One who is rightly called Savior because he saves us from the consequences of our sins. He is the One who brings the lost back to the Father. No wonder the Scriptures speak of our "great salvation" (Hebrews 2:3).

## Brought Back to God

"Reconciliation" is a word that beats with hope for those forgiven. Reconciliation speaks of friendship where enmity, strife, and hostility once existed. Our sins not only alienated us from God, but also rendered us powerless to do anything about the situation. If enmity is to be replaced with friendship, if sin is to be replaced with pardon, if the lost are to be brought back to God, then God must take the initiative. And he did: Through the death of Jesus, God reconciled us to himself (Romans 5:6-10).

Paul reminded the Colossian Christians of what their spiritual condition once was and of what it had become since their conversion to Jesus: "Once you were alienated from God and were enemies in your minds because of your evil behavior. But now he has reconciled you by Christ's physical body through death to present you holy in his sight, without blemish and free from accusation" (Colossians 1:21,22).

What is true about the Colossians is also true for all who belong to Jesus. Three points highlight Paul's remarks: 1) God does the reconciling; 2) the death of Christ makes reconciliation possible; 3) reconciliation enables Christians to be presented to God holy, without blemish, and free from accusation. These blessings are not of our own making. "All this is from God," Paul says, "who reconciled us to himself through Christ." Reconciliation is the result of God "not counting men's sins against them" (2 Corinthians 5:18,19). Every taint of sin that once offended God has been removed by Jesus.

It has not surprised me over the past 20 years of my ministry to hear people express astonishment at what the true gospel says. It has not been unusual for them to say in effect, "It's too good to be true; there must be a catch to it." If such blessings were a result of our own efforts, then I could understand people's hesitation to believe them. But when our faith is focused on Jesus, then doubt is replaced with confident expectation. Scripture declares, "For Christ did not enter a man-made sanctuary that was only a copy of the true one; he entered heaven itself, now to appear for us in God's presence" (Hebrews 9:24).

We need to pause a little to draw our breath at the wonder of what this Scripture teaches us. Unlike the sacrifices offered by the priests in the temple in Jerusalem, Jesus as our sacrifice entered into the presence of God in heaven for us. It is those two small words "for us" that guarantee our home in heaven when we die. Because I belong to Jesus, I know that when I die he will take me to heaven. I know that I am a sinner, but I also know that I have a Savior. Furthermore, I know that when the Father accepted Jesus, he accepted all those whom Jesus represents. That includes me! Jesus did not have to spend time in purgatory before the Father would accept him, and neither will I. What is true for Christ is also true for those who are Christ's. The purification we need to enter heaven was achieved by Christ's death, not by the flames of purgatory.

It was this truth that enabled Paul to tell the Roman Christians, "We have peace with God through our Lord Jesus Christ" (Romans 5:1). Peace with God is not a future promise; it is here and now. Peace has nothing to do with how we feel; peace with God exists because he finds nothing offensive in us. Our Savior has removed all our sins. Even when we feel depressed and spiritually low, our peace with God is certain because Jesus "himself is our peace." He obtained our peace "through his blood, shed on the cross" (Ephesians 2:14; Colossians 1:20).

## No Condemnation!

Paul's words add additional comfort when he says, "Therefore, there is now no condemnation for those who are in Christ Jesus" (Romans 8:1). No condemnation! This is a declaration of our total innocence before God. In reinforcing this wonderful truth Paul asks a series of rhetorical questions, one of them being, "Who will bring any charge against those whom God has chosen? It is God who justifies" (Romans 8:33). Every charge that can be brought against one who belongs to Christ is answered by pointing to the death of Christ, which paid in full the penalty for that sin.

Let me illustrate the certainty of a full pardon with an incident that happened to me some years ago. I entered into a business transaction with a company and promptly paid them for their services. Yet over the next several weeks I received invoices requesting payment. Friendly reminders were soon replaced with not-so-friendly reminders. Eventually the threat of legal proceedings arrived. My repeated efforts with the company finally resolved the problem. (Their computer had gone wrong.) I knew that the company had no case against me, for I had in my possession a canceled check proving that payment had been made.

Likewise, Christians possess a receipt that says full payment for our sins has been paid by God's Lamb. Our debt is wiped clean and nothing remains outstanding! The guilty are declared innocent. How can purgatory be justified in the light of such an array of evidence?

Yet even at this point some are reluctant to abandon belief in purgatory. A common argument is that we don't deserve to go to heaven without first spending a time of purification in purgatory. The sincerity of such words cannot be questioned. I often said the same thing. I really thought I was holding up the honor of the Lord with my defense of purgatory. But such comments betray a failure to understand what the sacrifice of Jesus really achieved. Not one of us deserves to go to heaven; we all deserve eternal punishment for our sins. But God, in his great love for us, hasn't given us what we deserve. Instead, he gave us his Son, whose death upon the cross pays the penalty for all the sins we have committed. His payment makes it possible for us to go to heaven when we die. We have God's word that this is in fact the case. Don't doubt it.

## The Catholic Reply

What proof does the Catholic Church offer in support of its doctrine of purgatory? A text in the second book of Maccabees is the most popular proof text used to justify purgatory. It says, "It is therefore a holy and a wholesome thought to pray for the dead that they may be released from sins" (2 Maccabees 12:46, *The New English Bible*). There are tnree points that need to be made about this book.

First, the book of Maccabees never formed part of the canon of Scripture. We have the authority of Jesus for this. He endorsed only the 39 books of the Old Testament Scriptures as canonical: "Beginning with Moses and all the Prophets, he explained to them what was said in all the Scriptures concerning himself. . . . Everything must be fulfilled that is written about me in the Law of Moses, the Prophets and the Psalms" (Luke 24:27,44).

Second, the book of Maccabees never made any pretense of being inspired of God. In fact the writer quite openly said that he hoped his work didn't have too many flaws in it: "At this point I will bring my work to an end. If it is found

well written and aptly composed, that is what I myself
hoped for: if cheap and mediocre, I could only do my best"
(2 Maccabees 15:38,39, *The New English Bible*). This certainly
doesn't sound like a man who is writing by the inspiration
of the Holy Spirit. No wonder this book was never regarded
as Holy Scripture! Yet the Catholic Church clings to it to
justify purgatory.

Finally, the book contradicts Catholic doctrine. The
writer says of Israel's slain soldiers, "It is therefore a holy
and wholesome thought to pray for the dead that they may
be loosed from sins" (2 Maccabees 12:46, *Douay Version*).
Those who died were found with idols in their possession
(verse 40). According to Roman Catholic teaching, idolatry
is a mortal, not a venial, sin. Upon dying they would have
gone to hell, from which there is no escape.

It is obvious from this brief analysis that the key proof
text in relation to the doctrine of purgatory is completely
unacceptable.

### What Are the Consequences?

Purgatory leaves little room for any real joy in one's life.
The fear of dying and joining the suffering souls in purgatory is ever-present. Even the most fervent believer in
purgatory doesn't look forward to joining the ranks of
those suffering souls. Knowing that one venial sin can send
you to purgatory is a frightening prospect.

I grew up believing in purgatory. This doctrine was
presented as fact, not fiction. I felt that my best hope of
escaping its flames was for the Lord to strike me dead the
moment I stepped out of the confession box. I gained some
comfort in knowing that should my poor soul end up in
purgatory, the indulgences I had accumulated over the
years would help shorten my stay in that place of torment.

One might think that purgatory is a medieval relic no
longer believed today, but that is not the case. I am writing this material in November, the month designated for
prayers, novenas, and Masses to be offered for the suffering souls in purgatory.

Another serious consequence of purgatory must be examined. In helping some Christians to see the error of their ways, Paul often pointed out to them the consequences of their beliefs. For example, when the gospel was being corrupted by legalists, who were gaining a foothold in the church, Paul exposed their false teaching. Some were saying that one's own works got one to heaven. On the surface this might seem innocent enough, but a closer look shows that this teaching was undermining what Jesus achieved by his death. Paul reasoned that if a person could be saved by his works (his devotion to religious duty), then there was only one conclusion to be drawn: "Christ died for nothing!" (Galatians 2:21). You can't have it both ways, Paul says. If we can contribute toward our own salvation, then the death of Christ was unnecessary.

To believe in purgatory is to believe that the death of Jesus did not remit all punishment due to our sins. In other words, his death did not get the job completely done! We still must contribute toward our own salvation by suffering. If one replies that his death did achieve our forgiveness, then I ask, "Why does one still need purgatory?" We can't have it both ways.

### True Hope for All

There is hope for all of us no matter how bad we are. There is no sin that the Lord will not forgive the penitent person, and none of us are so wicked that he will reject us. We have seen that, in his death, Jesus achieved for us a full pardon of our sins. Furthermore, in his death he reconciled us to God. He makes us friends with God by appearing before the Father on our behalf. The Father's acceptance of Jesus guarantees that each of us will also be welcomed by the Father. Because of what the death of Jesus accomplished, we can be presented to God as sinless.

The teaching of purgatory does not intentionally set out to undermine the achievements of the crucified Christ, but it clearly does so nevertheless. Because it takes away from the achievements of the death of Jesus, this teaching must be rejected in favor of the clear Scriptures which point us to

Jesus, who died so that we could be presented blameless before God, not because we deserve it, but because "he is able to save completely those who come to God through him, because he always lives to intercede for them" (Hebrews 7:25). Paul says that God "has rescued us from the dominion of darkness and brought us into the kingdom of the Son he loves, in whom we have redemption, the forgiveness of sins" (Colossians 1:13,14).

In the light of Scripture, can you think of one reason why there should be a need for purgatory?

# CHAPTER 10

# *What About Divorce?*

C hristians view marriage as a sacred institution, and any attempt to undermine it is met with vigorous opposition. God did not make a mistake when he instituted marriage; those who have been blessed with a happy marriage will testify to that fact. Marriage has many benefits: It can provide a couple with a true sense of fulfillment, and children raised in such an atmosphere are generally more stable and secure than those raised in broken homes. Society at large is a better place when marriage is lived within the boundaries God has set. Therefore the idea of divorce is like a red cloth waved before a bull to people who believe marriage to be "till death do us part."

### Addressing the Problem

Divorce can generate a lot of heat from God-fearing people on both sides of the issue; there is no shortage of proof texts used to silence the opponents' arguments. The Catholic Church opposes divorce and finds support for its position from the prophet Malachi, through whom God said, "I hate divorce" (Malachi 2:16). The words of Jesus provide additional weight: "Therefore what God has joined together, let man not separate" (Matthew 19:6). Armed with these two verses of Scripture, the Catholic Church feels secure in its position—no divorce, ever!

The reasons for God's opposition to divorce are not hard to find. The marriage bond which God made is broken by divorce, and the promise to live together as husband and wife is not honored. Divorce breaks the family unit, which is the cornerstone of a stable society. The effects of widespread divorce in a society can be devastating, resulting in great hurt for many innocent people. No wonder God hates divorce!

But every marriage is not bliss, and some people are tied to intolerable and unfaithful partners. The scars left on those caught in the middle—namely, the children—are all too obvious. A woman married to a man whose affairs with other women are public knowledge (and who might even be living openly with another woman) will be told by the Catholic Church that she is joined to that man for life. "Indissoluble" is the word she frequently hears when she pours out her pain to a celibate priest. Contemplation of divorce is out of the question if she is to enjoy the blessings of the Church and God. The obedient Catholic will fight on courageously day after day trying to resist the strong desires that can only be fulfilled by the husband she has lost to another woman. The dilemma is all too familiar.

Catholics listen to the Church's teaching on divorce believing that it echoes the voice of God on the matter. Over the years I have found that Catholics are often shocked when they discover from Scripture that God allows divorce under certain circumstances. "So why doesn't the Catholic Church allow divorce?" they ask. The answer is simple: The Catholic Church does not accept the Bible as its only source of authority. As a result, God is not honored by those who prohibit what he allows. Those who forbid divorce are not holding to a higher moral standard, for to allow divorce within the boundaries set by God is to do his will. When the Catholic Church prohibits divorce and says that God never allows divorce, God must weep as he hears what is being said in his name and without his authorization.

We must not think that divorce made its entrance with the advent of Christianity. Almost 1500 years before Jesus came to earth, God made known through Moses that divorce was permitted in certain circumstances (Deuteronomy 24:1-4). The chosen people of God had the provision for divorce divinely authorized in their civil and religious practice.

Divorce was not a provision that lay dormant; quite the contrary. Do you remember how Joseph reacted to the news that Mary, his fiancée, was pregnant? Joseph knew that he was not the father of the child, and therefore he was determined to divorce Mary. They were not simply "breaking it off"; they were getting a divorce and had God's approval to do so. However, Joseph did not need to go that route once he was told by the angel that the child Mary was carrying was conceived in her by the Holy Spirit (Matthew 1:18-21). In wanting to divorce Mary, Joseph was not going outside the bounds of God's will but was availing himself of a provision that God had ordained. Catholics need to know that to avail themselves of what God allows is not sinful. No one has the right to prohibit what God allows.

## Jesus on Divorce

Like all concessions that God allows, divorce is one that frequently falls into abuse, and it is against the background of such abuse that Jesus addressed the question of rightful divorce.

Some Pharisees came to him to test him. They asked, "Is it lawful for a man to divorce his wife for any and every reason?" "Haven't you read," Jesus replied, "that at the beginning the Creator 'made them male and female,' and said, 'For this reason a man will leave his father and mother and be united to his wife, and the two will become one flesh'? So they are no longer two, but one. Therefore what God has joined together, let man not separate" (Matthew 19:3-6).

The question had been put to Jesus, "Can a man divorce his wife for any and every reason?" to which Jesus gave a resounding *no*. To support his reply, Jesus went back to creation and cited God's expectations for marriage: Marriage is a union in which God joins a couple to each other for life. No one has the right to undo what God has joined together; that is the rule. But God has made one exception to the rule.

*Divorce can be granted only when one of the partners has committed adultery.* In practical terms it works like this. John and Mary are Christians, but John becomes unfaithful to Mary. According to Jesus, Mary has the right to divorce John and dissolve their marriage because of his unfaithfulness, and is thereby free to enter a second marriage if she so desires. Divorce on any other grounds is forbidden by Jesus. Should John and Mary divorce on grounds other than adultery and then enter another marriage, they do so without the approval of God (Matthew 5:31,32).

## Paul on Divorce

Unlike Jesus, whose discussion on divorce pertained to believers, Paul discusses divorce between a believer and an unbeliever. If this distinction is not kept in mind, a lot of needless confusion occurs.

The spreading of the Christian faith brought into the church many people from a pagan background. Some who became Christians found that their partners didn't share their faith, and so they wondered about the status of their marriage. Paul assures them that their marriage is valid even though one is a believer and the other is not, and that the believing partner must not put away the unbelieving partner simply because he or she is an unbeliever. Their marriage is to remain intact (1 Corinthians 7:12-14).

However, what is to be done in the case where an unbelieving partner deserts his believing partner? What is the position of the believer in such circumstances? Speaking by the Spirit of God (1 Corinthians 7:40), the apostle Paul says, "But if the unbeliever leaves, let him do so. A believing man or woman is not bound in such circumstances;

God has called us to live in peace" (1 Corinthians 7:15). What is Paul saying here? He is teaching that desertion by an unbelieving partner leaves the believer free to seek a divorce and to remarry.

### The Catholic Church on Divorce

There is nothing ambiguous about the teaching of the Catholic Church on divorce: It is not permitted under any circumstances. While annulments are granted, they must not be equated with divorce. An annulment is granted when it can be established that the essential ingredients for a marriage never existed. The fact that the marriage has lasted for years and has heard the patter of several pairs of tiny feet does not prevent Rome from granting an annulment, which frees the couple to remarry (or should I say, marry). The annulment produces the indignity of making the children illegitimate because their parents were never technically married.

For a church claiming to be the true follower of Jesus, the Catholic Church has put itself on the road to conflict with what Jesus, Moses, and Paul taught about divorce. Catholic teaching on divorce is in flat contradiction to Scripture. However, contrary to popular opinion, the Catholic Church has not always been the staunch opponent of divorce that she is presently portrayed to be. Her track record in this field shows a different picture, one that most Catholics are not familiar with. In *Vicars of Christ*, Peter de Rosa cites a number of interesting cases in which the Catholic Church granted a divorce. Here are a few examples.

> Two Jews, Isaac and Rebecca, married and divorced. Rebecca became a Catholic, while Isaac married a Catholic named Antonia in a civil ceremony. Next, Isaac wanted to become a Catholic in order to regularize his union with Antonia in the eyes of her church. On 23 May 1894, Leo XIII, stern opponent of divorce, simply divorced Isaac and Rebecca. This astounding case was, wisely, kept under wraps for forty years.[1]

Peter de Rosa relates how Gerard G. Marsh, an unbaptized divorcé, wished to marry a Catholic and expressed the desire to become a Catholic. His case was sent to Rome by Bishop Carroll to see if Marsh's first marriage could be annulled. Peter de Rosa comments on what followed:

> The new 1917 code said plainly that in his case these were no longer grounds for annulment. The Holy Office, ignoring the reasoning in the bishop's plea, changed it to a petition to the Pope to dissolve the marriage in favor of the faith.
>
> On 6 November 1924, Pius XI gave Marsh a divorce. There was no mention in the rescript that it depended on Marsh becoming a Catholic. To the canonists' astonishment, the Pope had simply broken up the first marriage. A valid, binding, naturally indissoluble marriage had simply been severed by the say-so of Pius XI.[2]

The activities of the Holy Office in dissolving marriages extend not just to potential converts but to people who have no Christian affiliation.

> No Pope had ever divorced two complete unbelievers. In 1957 it happened. On 12 March in that year Pius XII dissolved the marriage of two Muhammadans. The girl, having divorced civilly, took custody of the child. Her husband went to France, where he married in a register office, his bride being a Catholic. He was a prospective convert. The Holy Office, under the direction of Cardinal Ottaviani, recommended the Petrine Privilege—it took less time than the Pauline Privilege. Pius XII dissolved that marriage as he was later to dissolve five others that involved no Christian party.[3]

Pope Paul VI is known primarily for having given to the Catholic Church *Humanae Vitae*. However, he is not as staunch a conservative as his position on birth control would lead us to believe. He too engaged in dissolving a valid marriage.

> Paul VI took time off from writing *Humanae Vitae* to grant a divorce to two Jews from Chicago on 7 February 1964. The husband, having divorced his wife, had married a Catholic. He had no wish to convert; he was quite honest about that. He simply wanted to put his new wife's mind at rest. Archbishop Meyer backed his petition to regularize his union. The early church would have said that any marriage between a Catholic and Jew was a crime and a sacrilege; as to a second marriage.... But Paul VI was moved to pity. He showed the Catholic girl the compassion he felt unable in conscience to extend to millions who were suffering from the ban on contraceptives. That, in granting a divorce, he was contradicting a hundred pontiffs did not worry him. If Pius XII said it was all right, it was all right by him. Once more, he selected carefully the Popes whom he agreed with.[4]

One final example from de Rosa will be sufficient to show the inconsistency of Catholic teaching on marriage and divorce and the incompatibility of their position with their own history, not to mention with the inspired Word of God.

> A famous American case involved Consuela Vanderbilt, who wed Charles Spencer, Duke of Marlborough, in 1916. After ten years of marriage, blessed by two children, she asked Rome to annul her union on the grounds that her mother had pressurised her into it. The public was astonished to hear of Pius XI annulling a marriage entered into by two Protestants before a Protestant Bishop. Manning, Episcopal Bishop of

New York, called Rome's decision an "amazing and incredible" attack upon "the sacredness and permanence of marriage."[5]

## The Mind of God

With the facts before us, we can see what happens when the Scriptures are abandoned as the only source of authority. The Catholic Church has made two major errors. First, it does not allow divorce even when one of the partners has become unfaithful. Yet Jesus said that unfaithfulness is grounds for divorce. Second, its own history exposes its inconsistency in that it has granted divorces and dissolved marriages while lamely trying to maintain that marriage is indissoluble.

God desires that every marriage be for life, and would encourage even adulterous partners to seek forgiveness from the partner they have wounded and to reaffirm their marriage vows. That is the ideal that God desires. However, he has thrown a lifeline to those whose marriages have failed irredeemably. Divorce is available to them on God's terms. The sanctity of marriage is not lost when God-fearing people exercise the option made available to them by a loving God. To teach this is to proclaim the mind of God. And what can be wrong with that?

# CHAPTER 11

# What About Statues?

When you hear the word "idolatry" you may think of someone groveling in worship before a carved image of a god. We usually do not think of Western Christians engaging in such a religious practice; only "pagans" do such things. But a careful examination of the Scriptures shows that the practice of idolatry is a lot closer to home than most people realize.

Many Catholics would be surprised to know that the Ten Commandments as set out in the Catholic catechism have been arranged in such a way as to omit the commandment forbidding the making of statues and images. A comparison between the Ten Commandments as recorded in the Bible and those listed in the catechism proves this point.

## Do Not Make Statues

The Ten Commandments are recorded in Exodus chapter 20. The second commandment forbids the making of any image or statue for the purpose of worship or veneration: "You shall not make for yourself an idol in the form of anything in heaven above or on the earth beneath or in the waters below. You shall not bow down to them or worship them; for I, the Lord your God, am a jealous God" (verses 4,5). What God prohibits is stated very plainly, yet this divine law is never mentioned in the Catholic catechism. On the contrary, the presence of statues in homes, schools, and churches is encouraged.

Catholics are generally unaware of the second commandment because the Catholic Church numbers the commandments in an odd manner. If you compare the commandments in the Bible with those in the catechism you will see that the first commandment as recorded in both the Bible and the catechism is identical. However, the second commandment in the Bible (which forbids the making of statues) is omitted from the catechism. How then are we still left with ten commandments in the catechism?

The Catholic Church numbers the commandments so that the third commandment in the Bible becomes number 2 in the catechism, the fourth becomes number 3, the fifth becomes number 4, and so on. When we come to the tenth commandment (which forbids coveting) two commandments are artificially created: Nine, do not covet your neighbor's wife, and ten, do not covet your neighbor's goods. In summary, the catechism makes two commandments out of the tenth commandment and causes the second commandment to disappear without a trace!

Undoubtedly many Catholics would abandon the practice of making images and venerating statues if they knew that God had spoken so firmly about the subject.

## Why God Opposes Statues

God has not been slow to point out his opposition to the use of statues in religious practice. To make a statue of a national hero and place it in the main street of your city is not forbidden by God. But statues used in the context of religion are forbidden. God's hostility can be explained under two headings.

First, no image created by man can adequately convey to us the person of the one true God. No statues of God, however magnificent, can reveal to us the very nature of almighty God. Upon being delivered from the bondage of

Egypt, God warned the Israelites, "You saw no form ot any kind the day the Lord spoke to you at Horeb out of the fire. Therefore watch yourselves very carefully, so that you do not become corrupt and make for yourselves an idol, an image of any shape, whether formed like a man or a woman" (Deuteronomy 4:15,16).

Suppose you show a statue of the crucifixion to someone who has no knowledge of the Christian faith. What understanding of Jesus will you convey to him? What conclusions will he arrive at from what he has seen? The message of the statue will be that this man died as a defeated and rejected individual unable to save himself, a Jesus who no longer lives!

As Christians we know that the statue of the crucified Christ does not tell the whole story. It captures one moment in the life of Christ and freezes it there. But that is inadequate. The true image of Christ must include his eternal deity, incarnation, victorious resurrection, ascension into heaven, etc. But we would never deduce that from looking at an image of the crucifixion. That is one reason why God prohibits the making of any statues.

There is a second reason. Before long, man is found venerating the very image he has made rather than what the image was intended to represent. Look at what happened to Israel to see that this is true.

After the Israelites left Egypt on their way to the Promised Land, they murmured and complained against God and grew impatient with Moses. While Moses was receiving the commandments from God, the people made a golden calf for themselves. "They have bowed down to it," said God, "and sacrificed to it and have said, 'These are your gods, O Israel, who brought you up out of Egypt'" (Exodus 32:8). They attributed to the golden calf that which rightfully belonged to God: worship, adoration, and veneration.

Don't think for a moment that these people believed that what they had created with their hands was actually God; it was an image meant to *represent* God, who had delivered them from Egypt. Nevertheless, their behavior was wicked.

Guided by the Holy Spirit, the apostle Paul refers to this incident in Israel's history and calls it idolatry (1 Corinthians 10:7). To give veneration to anything other than God is idolatry.

On their way to the Promised Land, the Israelite people complained against God and Moses. God punished them by sending poisonous snakes among the people. He also provided a cure for those who had been bitten. A bronze snake was to be made, and all who looked in faith to God's remedy would be healed. Centuries later, when Israel began venerating and burning incense before the bronze serpent, the image had to be destroyed (2 Kings 18:4). Why? Because the people were giving to the image that which rightfully belongs to God alone: veneration and devotion!

## Detracting from God

There is no justification for making and venerating images. The history of God's people throughout the Scriptures shows that whenever they began to make religious statues it was a clear sign that they had departed from God. Such a practice has never drawn people close to God, but without exception has had the opposite effect. Reading through the Prophets, we hear them lamenting at the presence of useless images among God's people:

> Our God is in heaven; he does whatever pleases him. But their idols are silver and gold, made by the hands of men. They have mouths, but cannot speak, eyes, but they cannot see; they have ears, but cannot hear, noses, but they cannot smell; they have hands, but cannot feel, feet, but they cannot walk; nor can they utter a sound with their throats. Those who make them will be like them, and so will all who trust in them (Psalm 115:3-8).

> The customs of the peoples are worthless; they cut a tree out of the forest, and a craftsman

shapes it with his chisel. They adorn it with silver and gold; they fasten it with hammer and nails so it will not totter. Like a scarecrow in a melon patch, their idols cannot speak; they must be carried because they cannot walk. Do not fear them; they can do no harm nor can they do any good.... What the craftsman and goldsmith have made is then dressed in blue and purple—all made by skilled workers. But the Lord is the true God; he is the living God, the eternal King (Jeremiah 10:3-5,9,10).

God hates the presence of images because they detract from all that he is. In a very moving section of Scripture, we hear God urging his people to return to him. He sees them burdened, carrying their heavy idols—idols which cannot give them deliverance or the peace of mind they seek. God holds out loving hope to his wayward people. "Even to your old age and gray hairs," he says, "I am he, I am he who will sustain you. I have made you and I will carry you; I will sustain you and I will rescue you" (Isaiah 46:4). What a wonderful promise—if the people, instead of carrying their heavy gods, will turn back to God, he will once again carry his people! Lifeless statues cannot carry us, but God can.

One author perfectly captures the heart of the Lord in his short piece.

### *Footprints*

One night a man had a dream: He was walking along a beach with the Lord. Across the sky flashed scenes from his life. In each scene he noticed two sets of footprints in the sand: one belonging to him, and the other to the Lord.

When the last scene of his life flashed before him, he looked back at the footprints in the sand. He noticed that many times along the path of his life there was only one set of footprints. He also noticed that it happened at the very lowest and saddest times in his life.

This really bothered him, so he questioned the Lord about it. "Lord, you said that once I decided to follow you, you would walk with me all the way. But I have noticed that during the most troublesome times in my life, there is only one set of footprints. I don't understand why when I needed you most you would leave me."

The Lord replied, "My precious child, I love you and I would never leave you. During your times of trial and suffering, when you see only one set of footprints, it was then that I carried you."

## Revealing the True God

The apostle Paul has always commanded my deepest respect, and his life has been an inspiration to Christians in every century. When my son was born I had no difficulty in deciding upon a name for him: He was given the name Paul. The love which the apostle had for God and his zeal in carrying out his will is displayed in Scripture on many occasions. He was a man who "seized the day," always ready to capitalize on any situation that afforded him the chance to enlighten people about the one true God. This was particularly evident when he visited Athens.

Unlike today's visitor to the city of Athens, Paul didn't hit all the tourist spots. Instead, he observed the religious practices of a people who worshiped and venerated the images of their gods. The Greeks, although a sophisticated people, were totally ignorant about God. Paul undertook to set the record straight:

> Men of Athens! I see that in every way you are very religious. For as I walked around and observed your objects of worship, I even found an altar with this inscription: TO AN UNKNOWN GOD. Now what you worship as something

unknown I am going to proclaim to you. The God who made the world and everything in it is the Lord of heaven and earth and does not live in temples built by hands. . . . Therefore since we are God's offspring, we should not think that the divine being is like gold or silver or stone—an image made by man's design and skill. In the past God overlooked such ignorance, but now he commands all people everywhere to repent (Acts 17:22-24,29,30).

What conclusions can we draw from Paul's words? He certainly did not believe that making images and statues was something that had God's approval. Quite the contrary: This religious practice drove people further from the one true God. Paul not only pointed out to the Greeks the error of their ways, but also indicated the solution to their dilemma—namely, the risen Christ.

After visiting a Hindu temple in India, I was forced to conclude that the people who worshiped there were engaged in idolatry. The temple was elaborate, with its courtyards containing many idols of various shapes and sizes. I watched people pay respectful homage to these images, whose help they sought. Many brought fruits to the priest, who placed them on a plate, lit a small fire on it, held up the offering to the idol, and then returned the sacrificed fruit to the worshipers. The sincerity of these people was beyond question, but nevertheless they were engaged in a practice that God thoroughly detests.

## What It Means Today

What application does the Bible's teaching have to our present day? It is still relevant because there are certain practices within the Catholic Church which are strikingly similar to those described in Scripture.

What conclusion would the apostles and prophets reach if they visited a Catholic Church and came face-to-face with statues of Jesus and saints? What would they think of people decorating statues with flowers, lighting candles before them, genuflecting before them, and kissing them? What would they say about people kneeling before statues in fervent prayer?

They would be appalled. Such practices would receive their strongest condemnation. Any claim that these traditions have apostolic approval and are rooted in the observances of the early church would be instantly dismissed as false teaching.

There is only one safe and right path for all of us to take: We must listen to what God says to us in the Scriptures and pray that he will grant us an obedient spirit to do his will. Like so many Catholics, I did not know that God was opposed to the veneration given to images until I read my Bible. Today I have no regrets about having abandoned these practices. I would say to every Catholic, in the words of the apostle John, "Dear children, keep yourselves from idols" (1 John 5:21).

# CHAPTER 12

# Back to the Beginning

*J*oseph and Mary had gone to Jerusalem, taking the boy
Jesus with them. Partway home they found to their
horror that Jesus was not with them. Inquiries among
friends and neighbors revealed nothing; no one had seen
him. The distraught parents had only one option: They had
to retrace their steps to Jerusalem in search of Jesus. They
did, and there they found him in the temple (Luke 2:41-50).

Is Jesus with us in our journey through life? Like Joseph
and Mary, we assume that he is. In fact we are quite certain
that he is.

However, when we begin to look a little closer we may be
shocked to see that we have been making the journey
without him. The problem has been created not because
Jesus got lost, but because we have wandered off the straight
and narrow path and have not followed Jesus, who is the
Way. Neither have we listened to the Lord, who gives
direction to our life. What are we to do? There is only one
thing we can do: Go back to the beginning of Christianity
and start our journey from there. To find Jesus today we
must return to the authentic voice of God speaking in the
Scriptures.

## The One True Gospel

Do you know what will happen if you go back to what the Scriptures teach? You will simply be a Christian, a member of the one true church established by Jesus.

I recall visiting Greece and going to some of the places where the great apostle Paul evangelized. I was struck by the notion that the same gospel preached by Paul in Athens, Thessalonica, and Philippi—a gospel that resulted in the salvation of people in his day—is recorded for us in the Scriptures. I can turn to the Scriptures and read what Paul preached and how people responded to the gospel. It is all there in black and white for any of us to read. The assurance they enjoyed in knowing that their sins were forgiven can be ours also if we obey the same gospel, for God has only one way of saving people.

Breaking with tradition, stepping outside the religious norm, and going against the tide are not easy for any of us. But when our beliefs are shown to be in conflict with the Word of God, we are left with no other option than to abandon those beliefs in favor of the truth.

Look at all the Jews in the days of Jesus who broke with their religious traditions in order to follow him. Even the apostle Paul had to acknowledge that what he had believed and practiced all his life was not in line with the will of God. As a result he had to make a drastic change. Paul's newfound faith in God brought him persecution and eventually death, but it also brought him into a right relationship with God. If we could ask Paul right now if the decision to change his former religion was worth it, we know what he would say.

## The Step of Truth

The world is not short of critics who are prepared to put down anyone who thinks differently. Christopher Columbus undertook his voyage knowing that the common belief of that day was that the world was flat and that one could fall off its edge. Yet in the face of those beliefs Columbus dared to be different.

In February 1633 the Catholic Church summoned Galileo to Rome to recant his "heresy." He refused and was excommunicated. What was this man guilty of? Rejecting the accepted belief of the day that the earth was the center of the universe. Galileo's studies led him to a different conclusion—a conclusion which brought him into conflict with the Catholic Church. Yet today every scientist accepts the view of Galileo. The point I am making is simply this: Whenever any of us chooses to differ from what the majority accepts as being correct, then we can expect to meet with conflict.

Let me encourage you to make the reading of the Scriptures a part of your daily life. This may be entirely new to you, so begin with just a chapter a day of John's Gospel. It will familiarize you with the claims of Jesus. If there is a Bible-study group in your area, go along sometime with an open and honest heart prepared to hear what the Word of God says to you. As you grow in your faith and relationship with Jesus, give to him all that he asks of you, no matter what it costs. It is the surrendered life that he abundantly blesses.

### Eternal Life from Christ

It was in June 1967 that I was converted to the Lord Jesus Christ, and today, June 1992, I am writing the closing words of this book. In 1967 I was faced with the decision of stepping out to follow the Lord, and I was encouraged by these words: "If you follow Jesus, you will never be wrong." Today I am as convinced of the truth of those words as I have ever been.

I have spent the past 22 years of my life as an evangelist, sharing the good news of Jesus with anyone who will listen. In the climate of uncertainty that surrounds us today, it is wonderful for me to speak with confidence to people about the truth that God has revealed. To those in the Catholic tradition I would simply point you to Jesus, and tell you to follow him. I have used his own words frequently in my teaching of the gospel: "My sheep listen to my voice; I know them, and they follow me. I give them eternal life, and they shall never perish; no one can snatch them out of my hand" (John 10:27,28).

Could anything be plainer? Eternal life, the forgiveness of all our sins, the certainty of a place with God in heaven the moment we die, is given to all who listen to Jesus and then follow him.

Let me encourage you to do what Jesus said, so that you can know you will never be wrong.

# Notes

### Chapter 1—Who Speaks for God?

1. *The Documents of Vatican II* (London: Geoffrey Chapman, 1967), pp. 117-18.
2. John Walsh, S.J., *This Is Catholicism* (Garden City, NY: Image Books, 1959), p. 181.

### Chapter 2—Who Gave Us the Bible?

1. John Walsh, S.J. *This Is Catholicism* (Garden City, NY: Image Books, 1959), p. 177.
2. *We Live: An Introduction to the Belief of Catholics Today* (London: The Catholic Enquiry Centre, 1980), p. 10.

### Chapter 4—Is the Papacy Taught in Scripture?

1. Rev. Stephen Keenan, *Controversial Catechism or Protestantism Refuted and Catholicism Established* (London: Catholic Publishing & Book-Selling Company, Third edition, 1860), p. 112.
2. Campbell and Purcell, *Debate on the Roman Catholic Religion* (Nashville: McQuiddy Printing Co., 1914), pp. 26-27.
3. *Catholic Encyclopedia*, Vol. XII, 1911, p. 571.
4. John Walsh, S.J. *This Is Catholicism* (Garden City, NY: Image Books, 1959), p. 160.
5. *The Documents of Vatican II* (London: Geoffrey Chapman, Walter M. Abbott, S.J., General Editor, 1967), p. 115.

### Chapter 5—Did the First Christians Believe in the Mass?

1. *The Documents of Vatican II* (London: Geoffrey Chapman, Walter M. Abbott, S.J., General Editor, 1967), p. 154.
2. *A Catechism of Christian Doctrine* (London: Catholic Truth Society, revised edition, 1985), p. 47.
3. John R.W. Stott, *The Cross of Christ* (England: I.V.P., 1986), pp. 264-65.
4. Ibid., p. 265.

### Chapter 6—Should We Go to Confession?

1. *The Teachings of Christ: A Catholic Catechism for Adults* (Dublin: Veritas Publications, 1976), p. 481.
2. Ibid., p. 482.
3. Ibid., p. 486.

### Chapter 8—What About Mary?

1. John Walsh, S.J., *This Is Catholicism* (Garden City, NY: Image Books, 1959), pp. 189-90.
2. John A. Hardon, S.J. *The Catholic Catechism* (London: Geoffrey Chapman Publishers, 1975), pp. 157-58.
3. Aniceto M. Sparagna, *Personal Evangelism Among Roman Catholics* (Missouri: College Press, Missouri, U.S.A.), p. 194.
4. Walsh, *This Is Catholicism*, p. 192.
5. Ibid., p. 192.

### Chapter 10—What About Divorce?

1. Peter de Rosa, *Vicars of Christ* (London: Bantam Press, 1988), pp. 351-52.
2. Ibid., p. 352.
3. Ibid.
4. Ibid., p. 356.
5. Ibid., p. 359.

# Other Good
# Harvest House Reading

## MEETING GOD IN QUIET PLACES
by *F. LaGard Smith*

When the clamor of life threatens to overwhelm you, come share a quiet moment of peaceful intimacy with the Father in *Meeting God in Quiet Places*. These 30 sensitive parables from nature, drawn from bestselling author F. LaGard Smith's reflections in the Cotswold region of England, will refresh both your eye and soul. With illustrative pencil-sketch drawings by English artist Glenda Rae, this special book is one you'll return to throughout the year for life-renewing insights to guide you to the very heart of God.

## THE DAILY BIBLE
### New International Version
Compiled by *F. LaGard Smith*

Unlike any other Bible you have ever read, *The Daily Bible* allows you to read the Scriptures chronologically as a powerful, uninterrupted account of God's interaction with human history.

You will see events from Creation through Revelation unfold before you like an epic novel, conveniently organized into 365 sections for daily reading. Gain a better overall perspective of Scripture by reading the Bible in the order the events occurred from the widely acclaimed New International Version.

## CLASSIC CHRISTIANITY
### Life's Too Short to Miss the Real Thing!
by *Bob George*

In his down-to-earth style, Bob George shares the road back to joy and contentment in the Christian life. Clearly outlining the common pitfalls and misconceptions that can hinder and rob Christians today, Bob confronts the question of why so many Christians start out as enthusiastic believers and then decide that Christianity doesn't "work" for them. He then provides the truth that will help Christians get back on track and stay there.

## HOW TO STUDY THE BIBLE FOR YOURSELF
by *Tim LaHaye*

This excellent book provides fascinating study helps and charts that will make personal Bible study more interesting and exciting. A three-year program is outlined for a good working knowledge of the Bible.

## LIFETIME GUARANTEE
by *Bill Gillham*

You've tried fixing your marriage, your kids, your job. Suddenly the light dawns. It's not your *problems* that need to be fixed—it's your *life*! The good news is that God doesn't ask you to live *your* life for Christ, but to let Him live *His* life through you. With humor, candor, and "plain vanilla talk," author Bill Gillham takes a new and enlightening look at the concept of your identity *in Christ*.